T0063278

A Modern Woman's Guide to Successful Living

7 Essential Steps to a Bold, Beautiful, Blissful U

JANETTE GETUI

BALBOA.
PRESS
A DIVISION OF HAY HOUSE

Copyright © 2015 Janette Getui.

All rights reserved. No part of this book may be used or reproduced by any means, graphic, electronic, or mechanical, including photocopying, recording, taping or by any information storage retrieval system without the written permission of the author except in the case of brief quotations embodied in critical articles and reviews.

Balboa Press books may be ordered through booksellers or by contacting:

Balboa Press
A Division of Hay House
1663 Liberty Drive
Bloomington, IN 47403
www.balboapress.com
1 (877) 407-4847

Because of the dynamic nature of the Internet, any web addresses or links contained in this book may have changed since publication and may no longer be valid. The views expressed in this work are solely those of the author and do not necessarily reflect the views of the publisher, and the publisher hereby disclaims any responsibility for them.

The author of this book does not dispense medical advice or prescribe the use of any technique as a form of treatment for physical, emotional, or medical problems without the advice of a physician, either directly or indirectly. The intent of the author is only to offer information of a general nature to help you in your quest for emotional and spiritual well-being. In the event you use any of the information in this book for yourself, which is your constitutional right, the author and the publisher assume no responsibility for your actions.

Any people depicted in stock imagery provided by Thinkstock are models, and such images are being used for illustrative purposes only.
Certain stock imagery © Thinkstock.

Print information available on the last page.

ISBN: 978-1-5043-3393-1 (sc)
ISBN: 978-1-5043-3394-8 (e)

Balboa Press rev. date: 10/19/2015

Contents

Author's Preface

Most of us scramble for things, accomplishments and assets in life with the ulterior motive of wanting to feel good, be happy, be at peace and feel like we are of value. It has been my greatest relief to discover that almost every human being in the world today is driven by a certain deep inner restlessness that they are attempting to satisfy. Many times this quest isn't achieved because it tends to be approached backwards. At one point I thought I was the only one in the world who was having this experience in my life and it felt daunting because I didn't think there was any hope of things getting better for me. Now I know differently and I feel that you and I are very much alike because we are the few who are willing to acknowledge our deep desires and needs but also do something about fulfilling them and closing that gap. The search for freedom, love, joy and wellbeing is why all of us do what we do. Yet in all of our doing, the very things we desire still remain out of reach. In my attempt to do everything I could, thinking it would bring me what I wanted, I have hit more landslides and roadblocks than the average person in today's society. Starting off in life as an underdog, the fate life handed me didn't indicate I would go very far. Born in my native African country of Kenya in the bosom of poverty and discord of all kinds, we struggled to survive through day after day in the slum. I missed out on so much — perhaps everything that you may have taken for granted. Yet, amid all the destitution and detrimental lifestyle that you hear throughout this book, *something* kept me alive – and I mean this literally! There were many occasions when I didn't want to be alive, but life had a different plan for me. Given the conditions that I faced, it became obvious that I needed to decide what to make of this fate, because I certainly grew tired of the unending turmoil and being nothing more than an uneducated slum child. As I defined a turning point in life, my approach was based on preconceived ideas that were all inaccurate for the most part, given to me by my well-meaning mother on what it takes to be successful and have food, shelter, money and education. The idea of education lit me up, for it was the only thing I had come across that didn't amplify the angry, malevolent personality costume I was wearing. And so, in a mad rush to discover the big world and find success I took every route, path and method that I thought would get me there.

Many times we argue that our actions are rationally driven, but in truth every rational decision has an emotional attachment at its core whether we see it or not. I certainly didn't see it or believe in any of that. I didn't believe in anything except the fact that I was breathing and my heart was beating. From where I stand now, it is hard to say how I managed to live with so much anger and hatred for myself, for the world, for everyone. I have somehow disconnected from what those in my presence used to call the "ice princess". I now have trouble believing that she was me—but indeed she was.

In spite of my dedication to "struggle for success", thinking that this was the solution to attaining my best life, it didn't really arrive even years after I had stabilized and established my family and I significantly. There was something enormous that was missing and the path and methods that I used to attain what was considered by most to be success proved to be dissatisfying to me. Many who are trapped in poverty tend to think that freedom and happiness comes automatically as one gains financial security. I was very much carrying that same frame of mind and I always thought that having money could solve all my problems and make me the happiest, healthiest person in the world. As time went on, and money started flowing I realized there was a lot to life that I needed to figure out because I was more depressed, unhealthy, unhappy and more insecure than ever before. Something was seriously wrong in my world and I had no idea how to fix it. So, I have been that starving individual wishing for some food and money but I have also been that socially "successful" individual coping with life through daily medication, alcohol and therapy. In both cases, I couldn't make sense of life and I certainly didn't feel happy, healthy or free. Writing this book comes after a long period of reflection and contemplation on what truly makes an individual feel and recognize their value in life without having to sacrifice what they deem important. Society has done us a great injustice—especially the female members of our species——by promoting ideas, materials and information that disempower us and keep us living in a second-rate type of thinking. Everything marketed or sold to women is always trying to show how she is second best or how something must be wrong with her and why. Then, some artificial product is promoted as the solution to "fix" her. Consequently, most women go around feeling less than good about themselves, then wonder why they can't seem to find any good men out there to be with! There seems to be a black and white outlook on life which does little good for us, especially at a point in time when there are such great advances. And so I write this book for the woman who may not have had such an extreme life as I have, but who is still uncertain, unaware or unsure of what life has to offer and how to take advantage of all the goodness that's available to each of us.

It is certainly not written with the aim of garnering popularity votes because I think thought-provoking information tends to be misunderstood and feared by those who still prefer to live in comfortable misery.

My only intent in sharing my intimate thoughts and findings on the topics of happiness, wellbeing, success and having a great meaningful life—or what I call thriving—is so that a woman of today and tomorrow, who is ready and willing to express her own individuality can have the proper time tested and proven principles to experiment with in life in order to mine the diamonds that are available regardless of where she has been or where she is now. This is what will give her the necessary grace, courage and faith to own her unique and authentic voice and boldly use it to create whatever life she deeply loves. To know that even one woman might read these words and find her authentic beauty and voice and then shine her light in the world is the biggest satisfaction I can receive.

It has been a long, arduous voyage for this former ghetto child to rise up and claim ownership of my voice. This process necessitated the shedding off of almost all the beliefs and paradigm blocks that cradled my entire life. The definitions I had carried with me were pulling me further away from the wholeness, freedom and truth that I was desperate to find. I began to realize that many of the words and ideas that circulated around me as a female carried more negative than positive energy, and that this was detrimental to any attempt around creating new outcomes for myself. After all, universal laws dictate that one will have more of what they have, so if I wanted new and positive things to come into my experience, I had some major adjustments to do with some of the definitions that surrounded my understanding of the feminine presence. This is why, even before we begin discussing what this book will offer you, I would like to share with you what bold, beautiful and blissful mean in my dictionary today, so that as you proceed to set sail towards your dream life and thrive, you will at least not be recreating ideas you might still be unconsciously holding onto that do not serve your highest good in relation to these three words. Let's face it, women have been conditioned into viewing themselves in some really screwed up ways. It must stop now if we want to have future generations of women who are goddesses manifested in human form. So here are the new definitions I encourage you to consider:

Bold:
A deep knowing that something ineffable, compassionate, infinitely powerful, magical and life-giving is with you and moving through you with every action you take.

Beautiful:
A graciously contagious, energetic and radiant expression of the divine mystery that gives rise to love, kindness and a sense of connection.

Blissful:
A natural state of allowing, receiving and enjoying of all the joy, freedom, peace, love, health and wealth that life has to offer through the path of least resistance.

With this at the forefront of your mind, I urge you to give this book a chance and allow it to be the next clue that helps you fit your puzzle together. Life can be so much more than what many of us have allowed in and it is much larger than we have ever thought possible. Whether or not you believe or agree with my style or perhaps even these new definitions, I sincerely hope you will at the very least leave a corner of your mind open to the possibility that there is something of great value contained in the proceeding pages. It might be just one chapter, one statement, one word that could lift up the clouds covering your eternal sunshine and abundance. This, in turn, could send you off in the direction of all your greatest desires and total fulfillment. So, please be bold enough to explore the next pages as we discover how these words incorporated as living practices in your life could benefit you and those you love most.

My daughter has been one of my biggest inspirations in writing this book because I want to ensure that I do my best to create an atmosphere where she and those like her can thrive. We believed for centuries that the best we can give our children is standard education and material assets, but I think more of the world is coming to realize that the best we can give our children is for us to thrive and then teach them how to create it from a fundamental level as well. Wisdom combined with knowledge that is internalized and practiced is the only way I have seen permanent results that are effective and pleasurable being generated. This requires a lot more than just formal school or the right location and connections. My book will optimistically deliver a new path that you can begin to take while participating in setting up a bright future for all our treasured young ones.

The woman of today holds a very crucial place in the home, community, nation and the world. But none of that surpasses the vital role she plays in her own Self-realization, because with that individual triumph, she becomes as infinite, magnificent, radiant, nurturing and as revered as the sea is with all its power and glory. I see you in that light. Knowing the ancient teaching of Jesus Christ that the kingdom of heaven can be found right here, I can't wait for you to find your heaven on earth so you can share it with everyone in your world: you cannot give what you have not got. Successful living is what the great teachers of days gone by were attempting to teach us and it's exactly what will help you create your heaven on earth as you unleash your greatness. May this book and my words aid you in meeting that end.

CHAPTER 1

Introduction

It has been a great revelation for me to discover that our greatest joys are many times hidden underneath the garment and makeup of our biggest obstacles and problems. As the world advances in numerous sectors across the globe and we take on challenges that our ancestors wouldn't even have conceived of, one thing is becoming undeniably clear. The gap between scientific brilliance and that of daily practical living is ever widening, which makes the day-to-day quality of life somewhat chaotic and more destructive—even though the purpose behind all this advancement has always been to make life and this world a better place to live. Nothing can become better though, if the learner and inventor don't benefit and receive satisfaction from the very discoveries and invention being tirelessly brought to life. Only chaos, frustration, disorder, disappointment and a false sense of success can erupt from the kind of futile activities that defy the very nature of the human race as a whole. Though many still cling to the archaic idea that humankind is here to suffer and wait for a promised kingdom of heaven where all the good stuff lies in the afterlife, no greater truth has come to light and continues to be proven both scientifically and philosophically, than that we are indeed blessed beyond measure as a species and all the good stuff is found right here while we are alive. We are not here to take ownership, but to nurture and help expand the good work that nature has already done through individual specialized means that would otherwise not be present without our existence.

This truth is like a hidden ghost for most of us, yet it ever seeks our attention in whatever means possible, and at times, those means tend to be quite painful, horrific and strangling. Yes, I am not one to pretend that storms of life do not exist, or that we should just laugh out fear and ignore the fact that we might find ourselves stuck in debt, a fatal disease, loneliness, homelessness or something similar. I feel it would be a great injustice to the power that has saved my life countless times and taken me out of the deep, sticky mud hole that I used to call my life into the enchanted, magical place I experience today, if I didn't put down the words that will follow for you, my dear reader. These ideas and suggestions are not meant to be the only way that you may rise to success and find a way to discover your greatest joy from where you stand, but rather, serve as guidelines to one of the ways. I have personally benefited greatly from everything I share with you across the pages, and I hope you will too.

Never has there been a time when this universe needs more grace, harmony, happiness and love. Never has there been a time when you needed more love, happiness, wealth and peace in your life than now. It is exactly the right time for you to start finding your way back to love and learn to thrive. This is because the one thing we know about spirit or the substance that originates the animate and inanimate in this world, is that it *is* life, love and beauty itself. Is it any wonder that once you find your way and express life, love and beauty in your life in their purest forms that you will be as abundant as the nature you see around you?

Why not start today—now in fact—to step into a newer reality that allows you to live a life that not only fulfills your every desire but liberates your soul as well. This is why you are here on earth, and whether you see it now or not, there has never been a better time to realize your gifts, your potential and your role as a lover, teacher, friend, companion and leader. For many individuals—especially for women— it seems to be nothing more than a fantastic fantasy when I speak of such a state of being because it almost feels impossible to find freedom and acknowledgement in social situations we see in most parts of the world. Many women would argue with very justifiable and logical reasons why creating a life that is truly satisfying, loving and rich is difficult. This is but an old outdated notion that must be dispelled. And this is why I feel called upon to make this particular book available—especially for the modern woman who wishes to find her true value, experience real success and take up her most rewarding role, which will bring her the greatest satisfaction. Not by disregarding the past, and certainly not by attempting to alter the future with brutal force, but rather through the application and learning of the very principles that have brought forth every successful endeavor in life. It is my strong conviction that as the human mind evolves and matches the evolution and advancement of this world, so too will peace, order and satisfaction increase. Who better to be the vibrational heart of such a mission than you? You are, after all, the physical expression of the invisible originating substance that gives birth to all in nature.

****

Become bold, beautiful & blissful and experience how easy it can be to live beyond your wildest dreams as a modern woman.

For thousands of years, and literally up until the 19th and 20th centuries, we see very little information on women and the contributions that they have made in the world. Women were mentioned only in their roles as mothers, wives, friends, teachers and nurses. Things have gradually progressed to the point where women can get jobs, vote, drive and even have their own careers—at least for most of the world. Fast forward to current times and we see the extreme of the female archetype. The woman of today feels like she has something to prove to the world and it is always a battlefield for her. She feels strangled by men whom she perceives to be out to deny her privileges and personal growth. She feels unappreciated and closes herself up for fear of being used or taken advantage of as her foremothers were. In her attempt not to be anything like women in the past who seem to have been limited to being slaves and sexual objects, she has become very aggressive, erratic in her behavior and lost many of the qualities that make a woman radiate and shine. With that attitude, qualities such as grace, compassion, kindness, empathy, calmness and love within relationships of all kinds have greatly diminished. The lioness (as I like to call her), though becoming quite the achiever, is losing more blood than is necessary and in the process surviving on a very unhealthy, lonely, unsatisfactory aggressive foundation. While I am not here to get into details of the archaic female type versus the 21st century lioness, it is my intent that by the time this book draws to a close, your individual perception of women—as a woman—will have shifted dramatically into a more positive, holistic and beneficial manner for yourself, your relationships and the world in general. This is because I believe that while our foremothers played out a very extreme and submissive role which did not foster any long-term growth or mental evolution, I also feel that the modern lioness who plays the very aggressive and extremely ruthless role, elbowing her way in the playing field of life just because she feels it's the only way to succeed in a man's world is just as limited and unproductive long term. There has got to be a balance between both extremes for the modern woman who wants to have it all in life and truly live her best life!

Since everything has historically been recorded by men, for men, how much do we really understand about women and their journey? I tend to think, very little. As such, trying to go back and get to the bottom of things is not only ridiculous but meaningless, and with that kind of shallow pursuit follows the need for us to deliberately opt for a harsh, aggressive personality just so we can prove that we are not submissive like our foremothers were. Frankly, we can never really know what it was like to walk in their shoes! It is impossible to really know how someone else truly feels and so every assumption we make cannot be considered a fundamental truth no matter how hard we try. So rather than choosing sides, as I see so many women battling with today, why not seek an advanced level of awareness and embrace something bigger, something more whole that enables us to experience our own unique value as women in this world?

The big question that follows then would be, "Is that even possible?" Can a woman living in the 21st century really have it all without making the great sacrifices that society seems to compel us into? The answer is a resounding "yes!" The modern woman living in this century not only has a right to live a full, meaningful and successful life but has a mandate from mother nature herself to do so, and in turn, reclaim her spot as the physical expression of the nurturer and guardian of the offspring that originate from Spirit itself. There may not have been much recorded in the past on how to achieve this, but part of the reason you and I are having this rendezvous at this point in time as your eyes run through my words is because this is the beginning of a new era, this is history in the making—and you are part of it. The best service you can ever give now to yourself, your fellow women, your loved ones and especially the future modern woman is to make a personal choice that this will be your moment in time to choose to become your best Self. When you decide that you are a modern woman, alive and ready to live in the enchanting magic that is ready to reveal itself to you as you choose to live boldly, to express beauty and to share bliss every day of your life, not only will your world never be the same again, but you will be the trendsetter and inspiration of this new world order for women globally.

The flower is only beautiful and breathtaking because it opens up to the world and blossoms. It remains timelessly adored and always treasured because never has it given up on being its best self simply because seasons became unfavorable. Across time, a rose has always blossomed into a rose given the chance. And we never cease to admire and praise it for its magnificence. You never hear anyone mocking it for the short lifespan that it offers us beauty and freshness. Likewise, it never gives less than its very best during its lifespan. I wonder how many of us are roses that have become too afraid to give our very best because we worry it will go unappreciated or get trampled. Though it is understandable when we protect ourselves for numerous reasons, the price we pay is too high, for we also lose ourselves in that very process.

You may have had past experiences and even heard stories that left you feeling unworthy. We have, as a population, inherited paradigms and dogmatic beliefs that degrade and tarnish the value of a woman greatly. Somehow we surrender to that as a garment for life, never opening ourselves up again; but the truth is, we are losing far more in the process of doing so and it is up to us individually to put an end to it. Though the path may seem difficult at first—just as it is whenever embarking on something unknown—the rewards that await you on the other side are sure to go beyond your wildest dreams.

As I said before, I have discovered that in my deepest sorrow was hidden my greatest joy. In facing my biggest obstacle, which was that of releasing the hatred, anger and disappointment that I felt, I learned that despite everything, I had the ability to love. At first, it felt so foreign and impossible, yet I made it a practical working reality in my life and ended the struggle and strangle that had encapsulated me for most of my life. The start of that journey was by no means easy. It took effort and commitment on my part, but that was only a temporary transition which ended quite rapidly. Considering how deep in the mud I was stuck, I must admit, it took a relatively short time to unlock my heaven here on earth for sure! I wish the same for you in your world, and while there is much to be said still, I feel in my heart of hearts that you deserve to discover what more lies in store for you that will complete you and uplift your life. I know the pieces of the puzzle appear to be countless: how can you ever really figure everything out? Well, given our current state in the information age as a society, I think you need to make peace with the fact that you're never going to figure it all out. There's always going to be more of everything and one more big thing that you don't yet know being marketed to you. So, just stop trying to base the quality of your life on how neat, perfect and complete your puzzle is, and instead find out what is at the root foundation of who you really are. Then, pick the parts of society, resources and technology that serve you best. Once you shift to this perspective, you are well on your way to creating a life you absolutely adore. And I am not just taking theoretically here; I mean a practical tangible reality.

If you are reading this because you wish to create or revamp your health, or perhaps get a hotter body that makes you feel sensual and alive, or if you want more passion, more love, more intimacy, more happiness, security, money and satisfaction in your life, then you are in the right place because the content in these pages gives you one of the most profound ways to bring all of those nice things that we all love into practical reality. What's even more awesome is that you get to do it in a fun, creative, struggle-free way that is completely in agreement with the manner by which nature expresses herself. In a sense I am saying that we need to take up some down time with Mother Nature herself and integrate some of her working principles in our own lives so that we can powerfully manifest the things we want while still maintaining the harmony in our lives and in our world with others. In this way not only do we avoid getting into the battle of the sexes, which is so unnecessary for the modern woman, but we will become the vibrational leaders for a new world order that promotes the evolution of the human mind in a more cohesive yet congruent way with the universal principles.

Can you imagine how different your world could be when your health, relationships, career, business and family life all work in perfect order and harmony? Where you are in love with your partner, your children, your work, your life and yourself?

The great foundation that you want to establish permanently in your life to serve as a building block for any goal, dream or objective that you will continue to set for yourself as you journey on in life is what this book strives to teach you. Becoming a bold, beautiful and blissful individual will guarantee that you always approach life with great confidence and as a born winner, thus ensuring victory in all your endeavors. Please allow yourself to try on these new images on your own and check out how they fit in your life as you adjust and customize them to suit your personal taste. Learning the art of thriving and successful living is truly an art. And it is more than just getting you that end result or the success that you seek—it is creating a lifestyle full of love, luxury and meaning on your unique terms.

It is you being:

Bold- Having that deep knowing that something ineffable, compassionate, infinitely powerful, magical and life-giving is with you and moving through you with every action you take.

It's you being absolutely:

Beautiful – Being gracious, full of energy and vitality and radiating freely your authentic expression of the divine mystery that gives rise to love, kindness and a sense of connection to all that is simply magnetic and attracting to you everything that is pleasing.

And it is certainly you being:

Blissful- Finally being in your expansive natural state of allowing, receiving and enjoying of all the joy, freedom, peace, love, health and wealth that life has to offer through your own individual path of least resistance.

As the book progresses you will realize that there is a sequential flow that our journey together is allowing to happen. I aim to successfully and successively demonstrate in a simple way how you can rise into your mastery and become the shining star of your life's movie. This is why I've laid out seven steps that will show you how to create that solid foundation of your life upon which you can set up any kind of success you desire to have. In all my teachings there are five key pillars I teach my audience and they have been included in this seven step process for you as a modern woman seeking to thrive. These are: •Awareness •Assimilation •Attitude • Action •Alignment

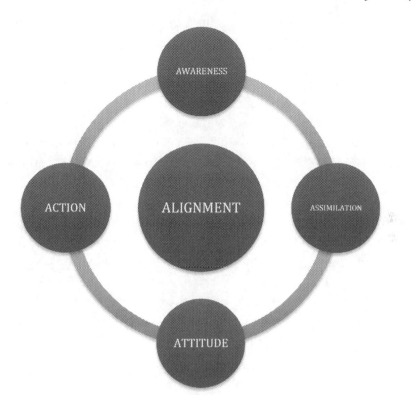

After years of personal research and study as well as testing this model practically with my clients I have come to the conclusion that shifting reality and altering paradigms in the mind are possible for anyone, regardless of what has been or where they are, if they only know how. These five key concepts of applying the universal principles that govern your wellbeing and success have become my personal favorite because they are easy to understand and employ. Unlike most, I am dead set in looking for the simplest way of making life work for me—and I hope you are, too. If that is the case for you, then the seven steps that incorporate my key model of creating successful living will not only be enjoyable, but will yield great satisfaction in the results if you follow through. These ideas work, but only if you work with them. I know many women resign themselves to a mundane, mediocre life because they feel alone with no one to trust or turn to, or because they feel things are too complicated to figure out and try a fresh start. Most just shy away from committing to a new life because they just don't trust in themselves or can't see how they can afford to pay for authentic mentoring and coaching. Well, I am bold enough to believe that I just solved all of these common obstacles for you through this book! Never again will you doubt your capacity to rewrite your destiny and create the life you know you deserve. Never again will you get stuck with no way out and never will you accept anything or anyone that makes you feel helpless and powerless in this world. You always have the last word in your world and at any point you can choose to say "no more" and create, manifest and live – the "more" that you love.

I know it is a big promise but the kingdom of heaven was promised to you thousands of years ago. Isn't it about time you claim it? It will take more than wishful thinking, but it can be done. That is how I have revamped my own life and I have now worked with many people who've done the same and succeeded greatly. I know if I can do it, you can too. The only question that is worth asking yourself is this: are you ready and willing to do this for yourself now?

Q. Am I READY & WILLING to start working on myself now, to create my tiny Universe as I desire it to be?

If you are sure the answer is YES, then you are halfway there. Now, let's roll.

CHAPTER 2

Raising Your Level of Awareness

If there is one thing we are certain about in this whole universe it is that we exist and we are aware of the fact that we exist. This, I believe, is one of the things that makes us a privileged species above all else. You know that you have the "I am" factor and even if you haven't been paying much attention to your "I AMness", I encourage you to bring that to the forefront now and consider what repercussions there are in this knowledge or lack of it, and of the level of awareness you currently hold. Without a renewed sense of awareness to deliberately play with, not much can be accomplished no matter how awesome or awful the material at hand is. With the right amount of focused attention and raised awareness, you will only need one idea, one concept, and your life could quantum leap beyond anything you currently could imagine.

So, before we start getting into details and specificity of your mastery and becoming, I invite you to just spend a moment or two bringing all your attention to your breathing and your heartbeat. Connect with your own self just by becoming aware of some of the biological rhythms that go on in your body whether you pay attention or not. Acknowledge to yourself that you are now choosing to relate to your body, brain and mind in a different, more positive way, so that you might begin to experience a happier, more loving and more powerful version of yourself. We are going to explore more about expansion of awareness and how to keep increasing your focus as the book unfolds, but for now, call upon all that you are—both the part of you that you know and that part that still remains unknown and trust yourself enough to "show up" for yourself so you can manifest your breakthrough. Without your mind's consent, nothing will become a reality because the mind only creates what it consents to as true for itself. Consequently, I hope you will not skip over the simple exercise of calling and connecting with all that you are, no matter how silly it may seem in this moment. Trust in this process and just give yourself the chance to see where it may lead you. The great gospel for you to take in now as you choose to deliberately design your life and attain true success is that everything you desire is already here. Nothing is ever created or destroyed in this universe and if this is still a new idea for you, don't worry, it will all make sense as the book expands. Albert Einstein turned this great revelation into a scientific fact and showed us that everything that is manifested is made of the same substance—better known as energy— and it can neither be created nor destroyed. What that means for you and your dreams is that how much you raise and increase your level of awareness will provide the path to your revelations and dreams coming true. It is all here: we just need a higher conscious awareness to bring it forth.

Things you must know before you begin

Whether you are into fairy tales, action movies or romantic adventures, you know very well that embarking on a new mission always requires you to gear up or suit up in preparation for the mission. Well, this is your time to prep yourself for the mission you have chosen to take, which is rising into mastery as a modern woman and living a bold, beautiful and blissful lifestyle.

Is the life awaiting you going to bring with it massive success, happiness, love, harmony and self worth? Absolutely.

You will be the queen of abundance and wellbeing with an ever-flowing supply for yourself and others. There has been much research carried out by experts which reveal that the things women want across the board generally include:

- Love
- Security
- Companionship
- A sense of accomplishment or satisfaction

Of course, this is very general, and every woman will have their own specific details, but I tend to agree with this finding because if we take a closer look at the genetic make up of women, bonding, relationships, acknowledgment and security have always been a priority. It is no surprise that even today this is what we want to have more of in our lives, with the only difference being that things are more diverse today. It isn't about men going out and hunting and fighting wars to protect the family while we as women keep the household in check. We are now at a place where life has become more dynamic and more expansive than ever before, and civilization calls for women to play a more advanced role. However, this doesn't mean that we compete for roles or that we hold up our fists to defend our worthiness in acquiring these new roles, but rather that we make the necessary mental adjustments and use the foundational elements and principles that have always made women symbols of beauty, grace and love, to step into higher and newer horizons in a harmonious way.

What does this look like from a practical perspective? Happiness and strong relationships will never emerge from battling things out with already manifested limited conditions. If you want to experience love right now in your life, you will not find it in hatred. If you can't stand your partner for something they did, mocking them or resisting and resenting them for it is not the best way to move past it. I hope you see where I am going with this. So many well meaning women have opted to use force and protests as the means of getting new results and changing conditions that do not serve the modern woman's well-being. This is what I call being an "angry peace activist". It gets you nowhere! If anything, it gets you more of the very thing you do not want. That's why Buckminster Fuller said we can never change things by fighting the existing reality. To change something we must build a new model that makes the existing model obsolete. For us to cultivate and manifest the success, love, security, satisfaction, health and relationships that this book promises, it is paramount that our approach is one that is fresh, in accordance with our true nature, and solution oriented instead of problem conscious.

As you will learn in subsequent chapters, there is a basic law that operates on frequencies much like the radio or television frequencies we are all accustomed to. And it decrees that everything has a certain frequency. The frequency of the problem and the frequency of the solution will be very different even though one couldn't really exist without the other in this dualistic world. And since the whole game of life is a mind game, you will now be at liberty to feel the profound meaning of Einstein's words when he stated, "We cannot solve our problems with the same thinking we used when we created them."

Something must change. There must be a new thought movement established and internalized by you before any real and lasting transformation can occur. In the moment you become one with the frequency of the new desire, the solution will instantly begin to take form and all that you currently have now as your goals or priorities or dreams will become a practical living reality. It is really quite simple once you get down to the basic foundational principles of life. Anyone can do it, but not everyone does. It isn't rocket science: there is nothing new that you must get or learn first before you are ready. It will take a short or a long time for you to manifest this in your reality depending on how much you put into it and really integrate it into your life.

If love, wealth, security, health and happiness are available in unlimited quantities for you and everyone else, why are so many women today frustrated, depressed, angry, sick and unhealthy? Why is the modern woman living in shame, guilt, fear and emotional loneliness? On the surface it appears that we are having the time of our lives with more freedom, opportunities, resources and more highly educated women for the first time in the history of civilization. We all have access to things that our grandmothers wouldn't even have dared dreaming about, yet even with all these seemingly wonderful manifestations, there are many studies carried out across Europe and America that prove that the unhappiness level of the woman today is at an all time high.

In spite of all the hype and motivation that society is now addicted to, translating information and resources into practical results regardless of the subject will always be easier said than done. The fact of the matter is, although the kingdom of heaven is real and available for your pleasure here on earth, you still need to make that quest and discover it. It cannot be brought to you by anyone else, no matter how much they would wish to do it for you, and there is no injustice, corruption or bribery on this quest because it is guarded and maintained by unfailing laws not created by humankind. This means that it will take your own personal determination and effort in the right direction to discover and uncover the treasures you wish to experience in life. Just as no one can ever breathe air for you and it is only natural when we can effortlessly do it automatically on our own, so too is the creative process of manifesting the experiences you desire. What's more is that this quest is more psychological, mental—and dare I say even spiritual— than it is physical. All of these are areas that human civilization has paid very little attention to until just recently because we have been so consumed and intoxicated with the physical experience. So in a sense, not only is the path one must take to realize their dream life quite unusual and less travelled by the mass consciousness, but it remains quite unknown as well. And with the unknown we tend to be more skeptical, doubtful, fearful and ignorant, making the whole journey mysterious and, to some, even ridiculous. So be forewarned that you will encounter obstacles as we all have when we first embark on it, but don't let that be reason enough for you to accept a life that does not fulfill you. The roadblocks and obstacles you will meet will not be there to stop you from attaining your desires but rather to help you expand and know more powerfully what you are made of. It is Self- realization that you are after because the Self is the real you and the aspect of you that holds with all certainty the kind of life you are seeking.

I always give very simple and basic concepts and suggestions for the conquering of this quest and the rise into Self mastery. Often I have clients who go out and create wonders in the world as they rewrite their destinies. However, there also are those who give up at the first sight of the unknown and revert back into a silent misery which is more familiar for them. I certainly wish with all my heart that you are among those of us who want to get the best out of life and accept nothing less. Many people—especially women—have resigned themselves to a life of silent misery or angry protesting and end up unable to create the love, happiness, security and lasting success that they actually do deserve simply because they just don't see how to attain it. It may also be because a lot of teachers of self-development offer great incentives and motivation for change and going after your dreams, but not a system that feels fun, simple and practical. My work is always simple, easy to grasp and practical because I am always more interested in integration than anything else. Please forgive me if my ideas are very plain and childlike at times instead of sophisticated and hyped up with the right "marketing" approach. It has never been my style and I intend to keep it as such. I feel that the more we evolve and advance in our understanding of nature and the Creator of this magnificent universe, the more we marvel at the simplicity of things at their most fundamental level. If we have made this realization through scientific research, don't you think it might be a good methodology to implement for your individual growth as well?

If you're still in agreement with me so far, then buckle up because it is time for you to take off with your dreams. Do not be fooled by the social setup that has left very little room for us to support each other in this day and age. I hope you have stepped out of the crowd that is always being wooed and controlled by a mainstream type of thinking which tends to be limiting and degrading—especially in relation to the potential of a woman. I am aware that many women don't dare create something new in their lives because they fear the critical voice of society: the "you can't do this, you can't do that", coupled with the inherited self limiting beliefs of not being enough, not being ready, being too old, too young and so on. The list is endless! Yes, all of those voices—including the one going on inside you—may not be in agreement with your choice to revamp yourself into a modern woman who has it all, but I wish to encourage you to be bold enough and overcome those barricades one by one as they come. Don't try to solve it all at once, just cross the bridge once you actually get to the bridge. Take it a day at a time—moment by moment even—just make sure that you will be among those who didn't stop when the problems showed up. I always say, you can slow down but please don't stop!

One of the easiest ways for you to really connect with this practice of raising your awareness and connecting with something higher than the life you've known so far is to start living your life in awe and bewilderment of all that surrounds you and becoming curious as to what story nature around you has to share with you. Many of us have become so consumed in ego-mind thinking that we have lost the ability to pick up the messages and signals that life is always trying to share with us. We get so intoxicated with human-made communications that we forget to request answers from the only Source that has all the real answers that will lead to our lasting success. I have personally altered my attitude over time and learned to nurture myself in nature and just find the miraculous magic and messages that nature is always sharing. The universe speaks to us, but it won't be in the language we have all have been trained in. This is one of the best ways to raise your awareness as you seek out your new path of successful living because you will understand that every living thing around you has a story. There is life in the flower, the fruit fly, the caterpillar or the trees surrounding you. The life in all these things that we very often take for granted is the same life that is breathing you. And just as those living things were intended to be here so that Spirit can express itself, so too have you been intended to be here for something grand. And it is ever seeking to express that grandness with and through you. So if you want to begin connecting with this expanded point of view, just dedicate a few minutes today to nurture yourself in nature: whether it's observing a plant in your garden or some flowers in your home or a ladybird on the path, just stop for a minute or two and see what message and story this living thing is sharing with you. It has a story too, just as you do, and it's impossible for you to know all the obstacles that each living thing has had to go through just to meet you in that moment. Yet against all odds, with complete grace and a silent power, it is alive – just like you. That power is all you need to tap into in a greater way to create a lifestyle worthy of your greatness. To know that you exist in this universe and deliberately use this knowledge in a positive upward progressive way is one of the most liberating feelings in this world. Try it out today in nature and see what that connection will evoke in you.

CHAPTER 3

Through the Eyes of a Survivor

I have always been asked by those who become acquainted with my message in whatever form, why I took up studies of the mind and the benefits that it has brought my life. My answer is always simple. I obsessively study and teach mental science and universal laws because it has been my means to salvation and a life beyond what I had once thought impossible. The materials I share with my audience are always more practical, simple and easy to understand because my main reference point is and always will be my own life experience and journey. I know many teachers in my industry who are experts (and very good ones) at teaching truth and transformational processes, and while I seek not to belittle them at all, text book materials and theories will never be the equivalent of experiential application. This, as it turns out, is what my entire life has been about. Initially, I did not know any of the awesome vocabulary that I have now nor did I have an intellectual systematic approach strategically woven to produce results. I was what we refer to as an unconscious competent, because to some degree I had been tapping into the very laws and principles that govern our very existence without intellectual conscious awareness.

Born in the gnarly bosom of poverty, superstition and isolation, my beginnings seemed to set me up for a life well known to those who had come before me in the same scarcity-filled consciousness. I grew up in a slum in Nairobi, Kenya, and did not hold anything to my name until I was able to fight for it or buy it myself. Feelings of fear, anger, bitterness and remorse for not having an opportunity to experience relief from the only life that was handed to me were all I knew. It was easy to define myself as the less fortunate one, the victim, the born failure that I was made to believe was my fate and destiny. The only desire I had for as long as I can remember was to go to school and become a cardiologist. I don't know why; no one in my family history had ever even heard of such a thing and I cannot even tell you why the heart was such an intriguing idea for me. Perhaps because it was the only place where I could feel something, except that mine was full of pain, hatred, anger and fear. But I mastered the art of pretending and concealing emotions all too well, because from my viewpoint at the time, emotions were a sign of weakness. In no time I grew into a fierce tigress, albeit a very young one, and was able to take up the role of breadwinner for my almost starved out family at the time. Not only did I play the role of survivor and head of the household well, I also eventually secured the basic needs that my family required to live a life that wasn't on the verge of poverty any more. I was a great success story for those in my village and as I grew, my responsibilities and ability to perform as a survivor advanced and social success (or superficial success) became easy to attain for me. However, when it came time to lay my head down to rest and recuperate from the hustling that I was so good at, my own demons came beckoning and it got increasingly worse as time went by. The success that I had been searching for with all my might came with a high price of emotional loneliness and isolation, depression, ill health and numbness to my heart, which ached and pierced the very core of my being. Medications of all sorts were my only solace and I willingly gave into this sacrifice for the happiness of those that depended on me because, after all, I was not worthy of anything in my own eyes.

It is true that we are our own worst enemy and many times we judge, condemn and punish ourselves a lot more than we do anyone else. I was a professional at this, yet on the outside I had perfected my art of "getting things done". To say that winter was the only season that existed in my world is an understatement. My sky had been grey and all things black and white for so long it became the only view of life that I had, and with that, all the dreams I had ever had dissipated. The saddening truth about living life without enthusiasm, engulfed in a state of depression, gloom and doom is that it becomes a coating that masks everything. The sky was grey and cold no matter where I went or what I tried. Every relationship I tried to have was a catastrophe and even the very family that I worked my butt off for was more like an annoying prickle that I had to live with. There was not much kindness, compassion, love or bonding that was exchanged with the very people that I was sacrificing my wellbeing for. But how could I expect anything more? I had never known anything more. I spent more days and nights awake than asleep, because sleep meant losing money and the onset of nightmares that literally chocked me to death. My dear mother, who forever fretted over me, once told me she always worried every time I left her sight because she never knew if I would have one of my attacks and collapse with no one to come to my aid (it was kind of normal for me to collapse and end up in ER). Even with all of this, I kept a straight face and made things work. I was okay with carrying on, even though I was dependent on popping pills while hating everyone and everything. I hoped for the best but expected the worst.

There must have been a very tiny flame within me that didn't go out though, even when winter and the ice age of my life took shape. This small flame must have been sending tiny smoke-wind signals through the iced walls that I had locked myself in. Though I cannot explain how or why, I feel that this smoke was the source of warmth and light that kept my heart barely beating year after year and provided a tiny dose of hope for something bigger and better in time to come. Had anyone mentioned this to me then, I would have scoffed at them and perhaps wanted to create a dramatic fight out of it as I was known to be highly unpredictable with severe mood swings. I was certain that my life was going to hell given all the things told to me by my mother and the conditions that we all had. Never had anyone from my family lineage been anything other than a struggling African. What was even worse was the fact that as a child I was very much unwanted and cursed, escaping death narrowly several times over. All the while I had a very African mum who believed that this was my destiny, given the conditions around my unwanted and unplanned birth. Although I intellectually stopped fighting this notion at some point, a tiny part of me was still that young baby who for some inexplicable reason loved books and dreamed of owning them, reading them and becoming someone of value. So you see, my dear friend, even though we have not yet exchanged names or identities in person, I know that you reading my words and thoughts cannot be a coincidence or chance. It is not possible that I have been blessed enough to live such an extreme life and still be around to share it with you unless there is some value I might add to your life. Indeed, I hope this is the one thing that I do before my last day on this earth, because without your benefit, your increase in life, your happiness and wellbeing, my mess is but of little meaning to anyone—especially me.

In my growth and in embracing my past, which I was far too ashamed of for many years, I have come to realize that we all face our own trials and tribulations in some shape or form. Though details, background and storyline may vary from one person to the next, there is always a story. Right where you are now—no matter what you are trying to create or manifest in your life—is the right place for you to be and this is something you must become aware of. This is your story, and no matter how bad it may have been or how bad it still seems right now, trust that you are on the only path that can lead you to the next chapter of your life where things will be as you truly want them to be.

I had to learn this fact the hard way and I wasn't aware that my future life experience wasn't set in stone. After all, when I looked around me, it appeared to me that it was. It also seemed that all the beliefs and notions that were passed down to me were the only possible reality. Being a poor African girl with no connections, money or education meant that you go nowhere and the best you could hope for is to get a husband and have many babies or get a cleaning job. Well, I defied that logic extremely, and I vanquished the poverty that surrounded us, but there was one poverty I wasn't able to vanquish in my life. It is for this reason that I wrote this book for modern women of today because I realize that although many didn't grow up without bread, clothes or a home and always slept with a full tummy, most of us silently die of emotional loneliness and isolation. Social conditioning has not promoted the qualities that our great-grandmothers embodied and so along with the information age and media manipulation, emotional poverty and isolation have greatly increased, especially for women. Feelings of being unwanted, uncared for and unloved are perhaps the biggest diseases we've kept "under the carpet" and they are becoming more dangerous than cancer and heart attacks. In fact this could very well be the foundation of such diseases.

I know quite a bit about living with fear and emotional loneliness. Whether we know it or not, it is in our true nature to love and to be loved. When we don't have this, fear sets in and many times we forget that we can love. An internal war turns into outward physical expressions which, as you can imagine, will never amount to anything good. Then we end up looking for peace amid violence and for love in arguments and hatred. That was my life, and I want to make sure that if there is anyone else who feels this way, they might know that they are not alone, and that all hope isn't lost no matter how deep the hole might be. It does take courage and a strong will to make the shift, but it is nonetheless possible.

My shift came after a lot of smoke-wind signals were sent out, and a messenger and teacher of love who reminded me that winter doesn't have to last forever even if it has been there for decades, finally got through the thick ice walls that had frozen my heart. To love those who do not love you is the most perfect way of demonstrating unconditional love. And just maybe that is what the world of today sorely needs. I truly was quite an unlovable individual: very flaky, erratic, irritable, melancholic and incapable of expressing affection of any kind. Yet this divine soul never gave up in his attempt to show me kindness, gentleness and warmth. Though it took a very long time and a lot of resistance on my end, the winter season began to fade away and, as if caught in a dream, I began to allow myself to feel something new. Something beyond anything I had ever imagined. I had thought myself to be very strong and fearless, but I discovered a new kind of strength that didn't depreciate my energy as was my previous norm. Instead, this strength brought more life-giving energy to me. And although my words are very simple and hardly elegant enough to explain the power that I discovered, I came across an observation made by the ancient Chinese philosopher and founder of Taoism which brought me to tears the very first time I set eyes on it, for I knew with every fiber of my being just how real his statement was. It is my deep hope that you will, too, by the time you finish reading this book.

Here are the words that today form part of my personal Bible:

"Being deeply loved by someone gives you strength,
while deeply loving someone gives you courage."
– Lao Tzu.

CHAPTER 4

How I Found My Way Back to
Love, Life and Having It All

"The hunger for love is much more difficult to
remove than the hunger for bread"
– Mother Teresa

This simple line summarizes a major paradigm shift that occurred for me because in the moment that the universe aligned me with these words from this blessed soul who literally helped reshape the world and demonstrated the power of what one in touch with infinite intelligence can do, I knew that I had received my next calling. These were more than words to me; they pretty much painted what I had learned in my life as a poor uneducated kid in a third world country and the challenges of rewriting my own destiny. In all the roadblocks, chaos, mistakes and challenges that I have had to overcome, none has been more challenging than mastering my emotions and practicing what I call emotional fitness. Turning my anger, disappointment, fear, insecurities and aggressive nature into my true natural loving Self proved far more difficult than manifesting financial abundance, a good home for my family and a comfortable lifestyle. I nailed down the material stuff that everyone who comes from the gutter is always reaching for, but manifesting love, kindness, emotional wholeness and peace took far more focus and a lot more support from the right sources before I could stand where I am today. This is why my observation of what

Mother Teresa said sent me on a frenzy of activities that took me off the thought plane of wanting to just show people how to create wealth, get results and manifest material stuff in their life as I have been doing for a while now into the very basic and very often unspoken foundation of wellbeing itself. We cannot possibly hope to have better futures and create a better world for our children to enjoy if we still go on with our lives on starvation mode. We cannot give what we haven't got and so for us to give our children a world in which they can enjoy what we dream for them, we must also instill in them that life giving energy and sustenance. We need to provide a foundation from which they can build secure and lasting empires, not weak ones that get blown away by wind or the big bad wolf. There would be no happy ending for the three little pigs if they didn't have one structure set up on a solid foundation with the right materials. It is no different for you and your loved ones and I believe the foundation can only begin from the elimination of the poverty that destroys the world more dramatically than that of food shortage. How do I know this? It took me a relatively short time before I trained myself in the necessary survival skills needed to ensure that I got what I wanted no matter what. I have always been an action driven, all or nothing type of personality and I had everything to lose if I didn't fight till the end, so I perfected the art of battle just so I could have food on the plate for my family and I. Results have always been my thing even from a very basic level and so I managed to eliminate the poverty of bread, but not the poverty of love.

I moved so far away from wellbeing, that not only was my health compromised but I completely lost the innocence and memory of love and wholeness that we are all born with. With a frozen heart in my iced kingdom, only winter was welcome in my world and the only way I could feel myself as being alive was through the chaos, pain and endless turmoil which I created almost by default. All that changed when the winter season finally caved and gave way to spring, and eventually, a warm summer with flowers blossoming all around me as the sun's ray reflected on the clear calm waters that once formed the cold ice that was my life. A breathtaking diamond dance could be seen on the surface of the water which now sparkled with delight and joy as did my heart and soul. I was finally freed from my bondage and filled with warmth to my soul's delight. It was as though daylight had finally dawned in my world as the darkness handed over the podium to the light and made peace with this magnificent manifestation. It was no longer about rivalry or judgment but rather unification and an acceptance of all that was, with an embracing of all that is and will continue to be.

It is hard to explain in detail how one feels in such a state of being, for the most transformational times in any individual can never be captured by words. That is why I like to say words don't teach—only experience does. It is up to you to relate as much as you can through these words and apply them in your life so you might capture the spirit of this message and know for the very first time how it feels to be quenched of the thirst that has humanity chasing ghosts. Mine came in small doses and eventually led to my full realization and awakening. Though every individual is unique in his or her process of transcendence and transformation, it generally happens rapidly. The path that leads to that moment of transformation can be quite long for some. I was on that list, for you see, with all my acquired habits of resisting and fearing the unknown, my internal battle and lack of proper knowledge at the time made it very difficult for me to allow in my true authentic greatness. Although I had a loving man who got me to this place, the heightened level of ignorance that I still carried about my own self, coupled with old paradigms that were more destructive than constructive led me to massive self-sabotage that left me hanging on the edge of a cliff. I lost the very thing that had given me new life and a sense of hope for myself and was on the verge of getting sucked back into the life I had once defined myself by. There is an old saying that a baby once born cannot be unborn. That was exactly what I realized in my own life because in the moment that the sun which gave warmth, light and love to my world threatened to set, the risk of going back into the cold freezing world of darkness and battle was more unbearable than losing my life. It's a funny thing about us humans, when we taste a life better than what we once knew, it is impossible to go back again. The taste of this new found freedom and feeling of what I at that time couldn't understand as being in love became my new obsession. I wanted to feel that way once more, with or without my teacher. I was angry at him and myself for losing everything he had given me, but as with every student I was yet to learn that this was just the beginning and the unfolding of the path to my own mastery and Self- realization.

Lo and behold, I picked up my fighting gloves once more—but this time for a different cause. I was fighting to find love, happiness and light for myself in my world. At first I thought it was to be found in another man, but that didn't go down so well and I soon gave it up because I realized no one made me feel half of what I had once felt. In my despair, another angel was sent to me in the form of a client I had at the time who noticed how much I had lost my enthusiastic, excited and energized spirit in my work. She suggested I read a book. That's it, just a book! One that I was very reluctant about at first and it took a long time before my mind turned from skepticism about the context of the book into curiosity. This led me into yet another wild goose chase. Now I was looking for someone who would give me answers and tell me what happened to me and why I was feeling like a dead girl walking now that I didn't have this thing called love. One thing led to another and my obsession with resolving pain and emotional loneliness by getting rid of the idea of love and happiness (for in my mind they were bad for me and the genesis of my problems) ended up paving the way for all the studies, research, training and intellectual knowledge that I hold today. This is what allows me to combine my real life experience with the knowledge that science and philosophy have uncovered in relation to the human mind and its potential. As I got into the obsessive study of science of the mind and philosophy as well as interpersonal neurobiology, I was more interested in ridding myself of the feeling that had been implanted within me. Little did I know that this feeling was my own Self, calling me back home to live in my natural state. The rest, as they say, is history...

My life today is really a fairy tale because as it turns out, in understanding my mind and retraining myself into the best version of myself yet, I amplified my ability to achieve more, to attain even more success than I had before and my health and physical body have never been better! I am everything I had once dreamed of and then some. Love, compassion, kindness, a sense of balance and wellbeing are my norm. My world is such a peaceful place and I live every day for a purpose and with great passion. I lost many of the earthly desires that I once had, but this doesn't mean that I am a monk—far from it in fact. I am still quite the material girl and I enjoy living the good life a lot, but I am more invested in a higher calling and my joy comes from my ability to witness the pleasure and success of those I am fortunate to serve. It is by far a very different life from what I had planned during my early years when I wanted to be a cardiologist. But I have made peace with my past experiences and learned to find the good and the perfection in where I am today because as you are about to discover, spirit or the Source that we all originate from never expresses itself in any way other than perfectly. So there is perfection in your journey even if you aren't able to perceive it now; just don't shut yourself from the idea. I didn't get to wear a white coat and gloves and cut people open to fix their hearts, and I didn't get to study in a fine school with other fine students and collect papers with my name printed on them as my degrees. But having this conversation with you now and perhaps bringing a sense of hope, and certainly sending a deep transcending feeling of love to you so you may know that you aren't alone if things feel messed up and hard right now—that sounds like a pretty awesome alternative and one that I feel more fulfilled by.

There is a way in which you can have it all; in fact, you are here to do just that. But you need to make sure it's on your own terms and is authentic to your true nature because that is the only way it can be lasting and satisfying for you. The life you are living is for you and not against you, but you need to be in your best spot if you are going to have it be so. The biggest challenge posed today by the modern woman who wants to be happy and have love, wealth and health is how to find that spot or even where to begin. The most powerful starting point for all of us as individuals and especially as women is through a renewed and upgraded understanding of love. Cultivating love and sharing it is essential, because as it turns out, this powerful awareness is like a magnet that attracts everything to it and a subtle glue which holds the entire universe together. It must become our new desire to seed love in our families, relationships, community, workplace and the world. But we cannot give what we do not have, so it is only logical that we figure out a way to nurture it from within and give it to our own self first and then share it with everyone. I can guarantee that there is a changeless eternal law that effects always follow causes. If you want to have more love, passion, excitement, satisfaction and bliss in your life—and especially in the relationships you adore—you must initiate a cause that will bring about this effect. That is how you can guarantee your love and happiness now and in the future. That is how I found my way back into true love and authentic power in my life. Although I didn't do it all by myself and I can certainly praise the man who played a very significant role in my awakening, I was still and always will be the determining factor. This book strives to act as a guide that will help you bring out the beautiful sunrise in your world, and I am certainly here to walk by your side and hold your hand through it all, but it will always come down to you. That is how powerful you are!

As for my fairy tale story, it's still in the making as I always say. My heaven on earth continues to flourish and produce more beauty as I continue to increase my boldness, beauty and bliss, as will you, I assume. And as the story goes, my divine soul wasn't lost after all!

I once attended a seminar hosted by one of the best spiritual teachers of our time who said that in God's world, nothing could ever be lost because everything we know as reality is happening within God's self. So how can anything be lost? What a great relief it is for you and I to start living this out in our lives. Perhaps this would be an entire book if I was to expand more on it and how you can live it on a day-to-day basis, but for now I will leave it at that and invite you to put some thought into it. I not only understand those words, I live them. I am blessed enough to experience the magic of those words because I manifested back into my life the very same divine being that I was so in love with, in the most perfect way after all. As I said, Spirit never expresses itself in any other way other than perfectly, once you choose who you want to become and play out your best role in life.

Play sheet: How I found my way back to love, life and having it all

••• Think of love and the role it plays in your life today. Both in your personal and professional relationships—but even more importantly, with your own self—how much love are you cultivating?

••• Think of 3 ways you can choose to nurture self-love and give love to yourself, starting today. Commit to incorporating them as your new lifestyle.

••• Now, choose one personal relationship and one professional relationship that you can deliberately work at showing more kindness and a loving attitude towards without expecting any feedback for the next 21 days. Keep track of any notable changes in attitude from the recipients you choose and remember to pat yourself on the back for having made love a priority in your world and your new approach to successful living.

CHAPTER 5

The Primer: Setting You Up for Victory

It would not be a very proper approach for us to begin our strategic journey into bliss, bounty and lasting success if we didn't map out exactly where we are and what obstacles might stand in the way of attaining our new destinies. After all, one cannot figure out the shortest route to the desired destination without first knowing the starting point. If you get in your car today (since most come with a navigational system now), it is certain that you can arrive at any destination you desire without any prior knowledge of the location simply because your navigational system has the capacity to guide you precisely to that destination. However, it doesn't decide for you where you should go, it simply follows your directives without question. What's more is that it wouldn't be able to get you where you want to be until it first determines where you currently are. In other words, you are guaranteed that it will get you the desired results of reaching your new destination, but only if you "set it up for success" by knowing where you are and where you want to go. Well, our journey into a more bold, beautiful and blissful you must begin in a similar fashion if you are to really succeed. Even more than that, we must be prepared for the barricades, potholes and winding roads that are bound to greet us along the way because on the road to Self-realization and mastery there is bound to be adventure. This quest is what we refer to as the "pathless path" simply because chances are, where you are going, no one has ever been before. Every destiny is always unique to each individual soul. When one understands this, problems and obstacles along the way take on a new meaning, and instead of being overwhelmed and scared of the unknown, we suit up just like the action heroes/heroines we all love to watch, and embrace whatever comes.

To have this level of confidence and courage is no easy task in today's society. We have long forgotten the time when hunting and fighting for survival and food was our norm and our bodies, emotions and social set up have dramatically changed and softened us up. We have become somewhat weak at focusing on what we want because we rely so much on daily routine as the mainstream consciousness. As such, our ability to be easily scared off and drowned in overwhelm and doubt has increased over time, which is why we are very effective at physical preparation for the next big challenge in life but struggle tremendously with the psychological and emotional aspect of it. The irony of life is, everything in reality is a mind game and the psychological, emotional and non-empirical aspect of any endeavor plays a major role in its success or failure. Basically what I am trying to say is, unless we suit up psychologically and emotionally first, we will get stuck at the first physical stop sign that we encounter on our pathless path because it will seem to be too much of a mountain to climb.

How do we go about ensuring that we are not only prepped physically with true bearings of where we are and where we want to be, but psychologically and emotionally equipped as well with all the right tools for creating lasting and guaranteed success?

First, we need awareness of our mental state and how our mind operates. There will be more detail about this in following chapters. Awareness of the mind that creates this mind game we call life and living is crucial when it comes to Self-realization. And in the mind we know that we hold beliefs and paradigms that help us have a sense of identity and serve as reference points for our capabilities and potential. Therein lies one of the major obstacles that keep so many stuck, sometimes for an entire lifetime. The beliefs you hold, whether known or unknown, consciously shape everything you see and experience in your world. They will be the greatest barricades between your desires and the realization of them because your wonderful mind, though powerful beyond measure and a true mysterious miracle, will never manifest what it does not consent as true for you. That is a huge idea to grasp, and it is a truth of life. When your mind consents something as true for you, it then must find a way to make it your reality.

What helps affirm what is true? The beliefs you hold, along with paradigms that are stored and passed on from your parents, their parents, as well as the environment you live in. Each of these cement the notions, ideas, beliefs and patterns you have been conditioned into. These are what have helped get you where you are now. The question that then follows is this: are they manifesting a magnificent universe for you or a miserable one?

If we consider the kind of ideas and myths that have been passed down from our grandmothers and their mothers around women and their place in society, I think you can agree with me it isn't a very pretty and proud picture. Most of them portray an image of inferiority, inequality, injustice and invisibility. While this may carry a lot of truth, just think of the damage it causes in your life today as a result of still carrying that hidden paradigm around with you. Not only does it prevent you from ever creating anything new, it also distorts your own self image and value. This is exactly what I grew up with and I am certain there are many of us being held captive by old dogmatic beliefs. There are so many things I thought I couldn't do, and it has taken me longer than it probably should have to get to where I am today simply because even as I learned how to survive my way out of poverty I was still playing small and hiding in the shadows as much as possible. I looked for the hard way out and trained myself to endure even the worst pain because I thought I couldn't possibly have it any easier. I was taught many things by my wonderful and well-meaning mother. There were things she taught me about who I am and what I was capable of which were simply not true! And what a sting it is that even today, many women still preach the same demeaning and destructive lies to themselves and their little girls. This is why it's vital that we bust some myths before initiating take off into our new voyage of finding our real Self and having it all. Though

I aim not to detail all the myths, I hope you can take some time to reflect on these and see if any new ones come up for you so that after take off, should any belief or old myth try to disguise itself and attempt to stop you from rewriting your destiny, you can be bold enough to see it for what it really is: a fleeting cloud in your clear canvas of life which shouldn't prevent you from experiencing the life you dream of.

It is from here that we will be able to release these myths and the limiting beliefs that we will uncover along the way, but I urge you not to condemn or judge yourself—or anyone else, for that matter—as you engage in this exercise. Anger, resentment or judgment of any kind will only amplify the very thing we want to deactivate. Find in yourself a way to cultivate a seed of compassion and kindness starting now— first for yourself and then for others. This is part of the process of our learning to nurture the state of being that will help us create bliss and lasting harmony that is independent of others. So it is actually a great exercise for you to start observing more keenly what kind of thought patterns and beliefs are running your life and how you can learn to treat yourself the way you wish others to treat you—especially when you are not at your best. This will take much vulnerability, but hey, you are a modern woman seeking to excel— and it's ok to be vulnerable because as you will see, paradoxically speaking, it is what makes you strong.

Play sheet: Setting You Up for Your Victory

Before you go to the next chapter and learn about five of the myths I had to release and ones I feel are most common across many cultures, I want to invite you to grab a pen and journal or paper now and see if you can start to recognize some thoughts and feelings that might be holding you back from having this life we've been talking about.

•••What could be a reason or two, or three, that you are still living a life that doesn't bring you joy, love, wealth and abundance on your own terms? When you look at these reasons, why are you holding on to them?

This is huge and really important to priming your success and ability to come out and shine. Be daring with yourself and see what comes up, then join me on the next few pages as we bust out some more myths and cleanse our connection to the source of our greatness. You're well on your way just by taking this step and I am already so proud of you.

CHAPTER 6

Dissolving Myths That Keep Us From Love, Life and Having It All

And here we go! There is nothing gorgeous or even sexy about this part of our journey, but we can still approach it in a fun and enthusiastic way. Imagine that you are a beautiful garden growing the most magical flowers ever, but weeds have been choking your flowers up and preventing them from blossoming and flourishing as they should. Like a good farmer, you're about to happily, lovingly solve this issue in the most productive and harmonious way possible. Uprooting them with caution, care and focus so that new a space is created and a greater harvest is guaranteed in this beautiful garden of your life. Rather than go in disappointed that you might have some or all these myths holding you back, keep that metaphor in mind—it works wonders every time for the light-hearted!

Myth No.1

"It's a man's world and women can't get equal opportunities because men don't let them."

Seriously, how many times have you heard some version of that statement coming out of the mouth of a woman? It doesn't matter whether it's a First World country or a Third World country, I can assure you after being exposed to so many different cultures, I have heard at least one woman affirm this as a fact in every one of them. I used to be one of these women, by the way. My mother and her mother all bought into that same script even though they were born and raised in the red soil of Africa. Now I know that in almost all countries in Europe and America women have had a very hard time speaking their truth. I know being outspoken or being seen was a taboo in the past. The women who dared demonstrate their boldness were often stoned to death or cast out. Individuality for women was something that was so risky that it was very often life threatening, and we all know of stories of women who died in the process. In countries in Africa or the Middle East the cases are even worse. A woman was more or less the same as furniture in the home. Where I come from, women had a price tag that husbands eagerly negotiated and paid. We call it a dowry and once the deal is done and price is paid it was a non-refundable sale both ways! What's even crazier is that this absurd tradition of selling women to men still goes on in many places. In spite of the fact that we are in a new era, there are countless women still being traded. Need I say more? In all of this, we can certainly see where the value, worth and sense of identity for a woman got tarnished and as time has progressed we've inherited outworn ideas that today only block our chances of creating new experiences.

The idea that today's modern man is sabotaging women's success is not only inaccurate but extremely vicious on our part because the fact that we hold that perspective and belief shows the kind of thinking patterns we still have ruling our minds. And as I mentioned before, the mind can only create what it consents to as true. It will be impossible to create harmony with our male counterparts in the workplace as well as at home when we still hold this view.

I am by no means justifying the actions of a man who is ignorant, aggressive, abusive and so on. In fact, if you know much about my story growing up as a fragile girl in my society, it would be evident that my traumatic experiences with men were enough to make me a man hater all my life. Yet here I soberly stand determined to get a point across that

I believe is truth. The man of today who is worth the time and energy of the modern woman wants nothing more than progress for both of them, and as long as the woman finds her true voice and strength, she has an open playing field with endless possibilities and opportunities because (and here is the big deal) the opportunities are not determined by men. Men are not the source of our prosperity or success and to keep holding them as our reason for being stuck is to disempower ourselves greatly. We have got to let go of this myth because as it turns out, equal opportunities are already here for us, we just need to understand how to realize them. It might seem like it's a man's world, but this is God's universe and everyone has their spot in this creative universe. That includes you.

Myth No.2

"I can only have one or the other myth: success goes to those who work harder, struggle and sacrifice a lot!"

The story most preached in schools, society and the world in general is everyone must work hard and struggle if they want to attain success. For women, however, it's blown up to a whole other level. We are told that you can't have it all. That being an ambitious career or businesswoman not only involves sweat, tears and blood but it also cancels out your femininity, love life, satisfying marriage and family. I don't know about you but this myth held a lot of ground in my world. I can recall years after my mother and I had established a relatively okay home for us to live in, I asked her why she never tried to find any work during her lifetime. She genuinely told me that she knew without a doubt that no husband would ever support such an idea and since her only destiny was to secure a husband and family, she never dared to gather enough courage to pursue any kind of work. In her mind, it was love or money but never both. Of course this belief was also stuck in my mind along with other horrible ones regarding relationships and marriage, but what an intriguing thing to see how far my mother carried this belief! And she could never manifest any satisfying opportunity to create her own career long after her marriage had failed. It actually took a lot of mental effort on her part to acknowledge and shift that paradigm. So many women today still carry that within them and they end up only creating professional opportunities and then missing out on love and family or vice-versa. Then they go around proclaiming that it is either love or money and both of them require great struggle and sacrifice. The harder you work, the more successful you get, but you still can't have it all! WRONG!!!!

You can and ought to have it all now. It is your birthright to have whatever you may desire and none of it requires strife and struggle. The idea that having a marriage is hard on women or getting a promotion is difficult for women must be thrown out the window.

You having a life you love, doing the things that bring you joy with the people you love most is the only thing you should be speaking of. And in all that, scuffle, sweat, tears and blood must never be entertained by you because as with nature, everything that is lasting and beautiful always unfolds naturally and effortlessly. Here's the thing, as a woman you are the symbol of Mother Nature who births everything into existence. Mother Nature never struggles; grass doesn't strain to grow, stars don't struggle to sparkle and certainly the sun doesn't strain to shine. Your place in society as you can see, is the physical embodiment of that divine essence that is Mother Nature. Therefore whenever you're confronted with thoughts of struggle and more hard work to attain something, remember these words, contemplate on them and then just observe the nature around you to find your true spot in this universe. You can have it all, in as much or as little abundance as you choose. The power you hold comes from a place that has been forgotten by most. Perhaps you had forgotten it too, but now you're returning to the path of your glory that will allow you to shift from struggling into success to joying your way into success naturally.

Myth No.3

"If you love the good life and want to be wealthy but you don't have a rich daddy, your only chance is marrying a rich husband."

Now, I don't know about you, but this ridiculous statement held residence in the sacred home of my mind for too long. I can't tell you how many times I heard this song playing in my environment and in my head. It became the only tune that I danced to actually and since I didn't have any daddy, I was miserable at the idea of marrying just so I could be wealthy. How many times have you heard this in your life or from women you know? What is crazy about reality is that if this is a belief you hold then whenever you look around you, it is certain that those women whom you see getting ahead in life will have the connections or the right husband. What's even worse is if you end up marrying someone and this is your hidden paradigm, you will also experience feelings of insecurity and inadequacy so that every time someone jokes with you about it, you will cringe and take it personally. Having spent a lot of time in Monaco, I have met many women who are awesome ladies but they live in guilt and insecurity over the life of luxury that they have. It expresses itself in ways that, to the observer, makes them appear bad and unhappy or wasting away. In truth, they are stuck in a type of bondage and poverty that might be just as bad as it is for an individual stuck in a slum. The only difference is, it's much easier to end physical bondage, but not as easy to end psychological or mental captivity. This was an amazing discovery for me because growing up as a slum kid I really thought the only problem in the world was lack of finances and opportunity. But as you will continue to learn, there is a far greater poverty and crisis in the world than that of bread and milk for all to feast upon.

This is why this belief is perhaps one of the most destructive ones to hold on to, because it's like a silent poison that slowly eats you up. I have always been an overly ambitious girl and always wanted the good life. But the guilt of wanting more and having to apologize for this desire to reach for more was a lot to bear especially because there was a point I realized the wealth and good life I was seeking wasn't coming to me in a satisfying way. As you might imagine, my beliefs were deeper and more rotten than this one—especially regarding the issue of relationships and money—so I know a thing or two about paradigm shifting on this very sensitive matter. Yet I can tell you as sure as sunrise, your wealth has nothing to do with the men in your life whether you have a daddy or husband or not. I had none, and I went chasing after husbands that I realized I didn't even want anyways, and it took a lot of chasing around and shooting myself in the foot over and over again before I finally stopped and asked myself, "Why is it that I can only be wealthy if I have a dad or hubby? Why can't I be the wealthy one?" No one had ever told me that I could be the wealthy one and the source of my own security and love. That was a life changing moment for me because it not only helped me release limiting beliefs that were giving me more of what I didn't want, but it also allowed me to attract the kind of men I actually loved. Don't get me wrong, I am in no way saying you shouldn't get married to a rich husband, I absolutely promote that in fact. And I am also not saying you shouldn't receive support from your rich daddy or whichever male figure you have in your life, but I am saying the perception and perspective you hold about it means the difference between lasting happiness and success and living in shame, guilt and silent depression. It all comes down to letting go of this belief and building a new paradigm for yourself that supports the desire to be wealthy, live a good life and enjoy luxury with those you have a relationship with. So, where is your source of wealth and luxury now?

Myth No.4

"You can't be a good girl and have it all."

I believe this myth is one that has been perpetuated by religion and the media in the recent past. The idea of wrong or right and good or bad can really sabotage a sense of worth and value for a woman. Religion seems to want to separate and classify the idea of good as being less materialistic and physical. This results in the perspective that the more you care about being beautiful, living a life of luxury, and enjoying an awesome life, the more you are a bad girl. The shy, altruistic girl who doesn't want money and only worships in church and never talks about sex or relationships and gets married only once and sticks with it till she dies and basically avoids all earthly pleasures is the good one. Okay, I don't know about you, but I really don't believe this is the image of a good girl—if there is such a thing. We need to stop feeling ashamed of our bodies and condemning those who are flagrant and conspicuous about theirs and start practicing self-care and self-nurturing. A beautiful, elegant, radiant lady is the face of the reinvented modern-day woman and she is never shy or uncomfortable with her sensuality. She neither avoids earthly pleasures nor excessively overindulges in vanity affairs that are detrimental to her own worth and sense of value. She is exactly as nature is: abundant, graceful, loving, magnificent, sexy, enchanting, beautiful, bold and content. The idea that you are either spiritual or materialistic is fast fading as the whole world awakens to a new era, and a new thought movement, of which I feel humbled and highly privileged to help spread across nations. This new revolution and evolution for us all as a human species is the understanding that we are supposed to embrace both the spiritual and material in our human journeys and that one aspect without the other creates disharmony. So you stepping up your game and becoming a modern woman of excellence in society requires you to give up the good girl/bad girl approach and reach for something higher where you realize that, in fact, you can have it all, you deserve to have it all and you are always, in every case a good girl.

Myth No.5

"To be successful you must be more serious, more aggressive, less feminine and beautiful."

This myth seems to be holding strong still, especially in the professional world where many modern women want to be. Let's see if we can dilute it just a bit and make it soft enough for you to release. It is certainly true that for a very long time only men led the workplace and enhanced governance and democracy. In fact, in wanting to have more knowledge of women's journey through history, I realized there really hasn't been much recorded. I suppose this is because no one really cared enough to document the activities of the home, which was the domain of females. Civilization as a whole was more concerned about power, politics, positions, constitutions and so on. In a sense we really can't have a very accurate bearing on the history of "the woman" other than the fact that she wasn't in the picture of what was considered "serious business". Fast forward civilization and modernization and we begin to see women stepping into the playing field of serious business. This took a lot of courage for sure and without a doubt, these women experienced lots of criticism and discouragement. But here is the thing, human beings do not judge and discourage because of gender issues, they judge, discourage and fear anything new that demands mental adjustment. I strongly believe that men had an issue with the age of the free spirited, self-accomplished working woman simply because it was an unknown and demanded that they change perspective. We ought to give them a break because we all know how it feels to fear the unknown; we do it all the time as part of our social conditioning. That's why the economic crisis in Italy has taken so long to recover because it is hard to embrace the unknown and flow with it. But it isn't just the Italians; many cultures suffer the same. So when it comes to the men-women paradigm shift, it was bound to be exactly the same.

The ladies who took on the challenge approached the man's world and the man's game with a forceful "manly" approach and I must say, they did a great job because look where we are today thanks to them attacking/playing the game like men. But this isn't sustainable at all. Why? Because we are not men.

God does not make errors, and trying to make him wrong because we can't figure out how to win as women is our biggest obstacle to date. While it took a lot of courage, physical strength and toughness to fight for our chance to have a voice, we now have the entire platform but we are more depressed, burned out, lonely and unhappy than ever before. It's absurd how many women are suffering from some disease or dysfunction at such early ages, all of which I am certain has a lot to do with the constant overwhelm, worry and battles going on from day-to-day. The woman is a symbol of grace, beauty, mystery and love that beholds the whole universe. She is the veil and the symbolic manifestation of that which births all that is physically manifested. Fighting her way through life just to compete for the pie that she now believes is limited and being kept from her by men completely defies her true nature and weakens her real strength.

Therefore inasmuch as suiting up as a man and trying to fit into "serious business" was a great way to set the wheel into motion, the time for survival based living has long passed. We now want to help humankind thrive in a manner that is appreciative and more life giving for future generations but for our own future as well. This requires playing the man's game as a woman. It's time for us to start being authentic to who we are, coming from a centered, grounded space that corresponds with our true nature as the female of our species. In this way, we will discover that our spot in society as well as in serious business has been here all along. For so long now professional women have emulated the image of men: very serious, aggressive, malevolent, ruthless, and less concerned about grace, grooming, beauty and etiquette. I think today it has become even more extreme. It has become (for a lack of better word), the Alpha Bitch Mode. Someone convinced us this was the only way to make it to the top, but look around you and notice how much lasting and true success those who are Alpha Bitches actually experience. We need a new system, a new approach. It has to be authentic to our blessed femininity, compassion, beauty and grace. That is one of the key missing elements in women's world today.

There are many more myths that secretly sabotage our efforts to enjoy a full life today. We are only awakening now to the possibility that we can indeed have everything we want in life without compromising the things we value—especially our unique voices. Outworn beliefs will give way if you are candid enough with yourself to allow the acknowledgement and release process to happen. Coating it, covering it up with makeup, or sweeping it under the carpet because it feels too shameful or frightening to deal with will only keep you stuck where you are now. This would be like putting a happy face sticker on your fuel gauge in your car just because you feel ashamed to acknowledge that you forgot to put fuel in your car. We all appreciate the fact that we have a fuel indicator and warning signals to let us know what must be done to ensure the car continues to run smoothly. So don't skip over this part no matter how silly it may feel for you.

It wasn't easy for me to own all of my messes and dark shadows. I had to be very loving and accepting of myself to embrace things that were disgusting to me about me. But I wouldn't be here walking with you through this, if I hadn't taken that risk, made that choice and followed through.

Sometimes it is hard because many of these beliefs are ones we got from people we really love. Sometimes we feel like we are betraying someone or losing something by choosing to renew our thought patterns and beliefs, but I promise you one thing: you are gaining everything and losing nothing by choosing to take this step. Not only will it benefit you and those who come after you, but even those you worry might not support you if you change will stand a greater chance of living a better life when you choose to be the carrier of this good life. It is yours for the having, but you must choose it first.

So many women are just scraping and crawling through life, wishing for something better yet doing nothing about it. Please don't be one of those women. Your world needs you badly, your loved ones need you more than you will ever know and your voice can heal, feed and nurture more people than you can imagine, but you've got to be at your best for these aspects to come shining through. Having realized and hopefully released some limiting beliefs is a sure way that you will be unstoppable in this journey you have chosen. Although you might find more obstacles and problems along the path, trust that you will have the resources, courage and wisdom that will guide you above and beyond. So take it easy, breathe more, relax more, send some more love to yourself right now and allow yourself to trust in your own ability to win in life.

We are at the point now where all systems are ready to go and we can dig deeper into the actual practical steps and systems that will help you become that bold, beautiful and blissful version of you. I certainly hope you are ready because I know I am. I hope you are not only willing but keen to give your voice the freedom and acknowledgement it deserves in an authentic, holistic way. And I hope you already feel unstoppable because things will always come up that test how resilient and certain you are about what you wish to manifest. Also, it is quite common for people around us to try and protect us by discouraging us from doing what they feel is impossible. Understand they only do so because they believe it is hard or impossible for *them*—that doesn't mean it will be hard or impossible for *you*. This is why I always say it is the pathless path and only when you get moving will you discover how easy it is for you.

If you have always wanted this life you are now creating but have heard things like:

- You can't have the money, influence and lifestyle you've always wanted without compromising your time, relationships and dreams.
- You can't build a successful career or business on your terms without being more masculine or getting burned out.
- You can't be beautiful, fabulous and demonstrate life mastery that inspires other women to step up and shine; no one would take you seriously.
- You shouldn't ask for too much, you must be humble and just accept what you have is all you can have.
- You shouldn't speak up. Squelch your enthusiasm and be more realistic.

Now is your chance to show the world how wrong they have been about you and what you are capable of because you can do all this and more in an effortless and fun manner that is on your terms. This book is bound to get you soaring in every area of your life and it is my deepest desire that you will switch from the voice of other's opinions to your own inner sacred voice.

As a result of reading this book or working with me in one way or another you can finally expect to receive benefits such as:

- Being authentically fabulous & bold. Saying goodbye to the feeling of unworthiness, boost your self-confidence and find your voice. This is what will be the foundation of your transformation.
- Changing habits and beliefs that sabotage your success such as, " hard work equals success."
- You will finally overcome limiting beliefs that are sabotaging you. Releasing the past is crucial so that you can leave behind all the "could haves" and "should haves" and then march forward in life.
- You can finally develop routines of self-care, self-love and self-worth because if you don't appreciate and value yourself, no one else will.
- Breaking free from your fears and insecurities. But more importantly you will become a Self-realizing being who isn't swayed by fear and doubts.
- You will recharge your inner power and stop procrastinating. You'll stop waiting for that mythical something—"when I will have this or that"—and allow yourself to excel and become a thriving modern woman NOW.

My work is really cut out for me and I intend to raise the bar for myself on this because I truly believe that you are greatness in the making. Now, let's go pick up those tools and the system to reveal this greatness that you already posses.

Play sheet: Dissolving Myths That Keep Us From Love, Life and Having It All

••• It takes a lot of courage and a bit of vulnerability to open up and embrace the aspects of you that you prefer not to look at. These dark shadows can keep us choked in guilt and a feeling of being less than worthy—or they can help us discover more of who we really are. Allowing yourself to own all of who you are and never apologizing for your ambiguity is crucial in renewing the mind and releasing past thought patterns and old beliefs, so I encourage you to give yourself a few moments here to welcome in every aspect of you – good and bad – and choose which part you want to show up as you move forward.

••• How many limiting beliefs hit home for you from those mentioned above? See if you can write a few more that come up on a piece of paper. As beliefs come up and you recognize they are constricting you rather than expanding you, make a conscious mental note to release their energy from your mind, body and spirit and create space for new beliefs.

••• For every belief that you release, write down in your journal a new belief that you now choose to carry. Practice living with this new thought pattern, read it again regularly when it feels good and contemplate the effects in your life of living from that new paradigm. Sooner rather than later, it will crystallize as your new habit of thought, so keep at it and trust that your garden is better than ever now that you've consciously and deliberately cleaned up.

CHAPTER 7

The First Essential (Part I): Getting into the Spirit of U

The Connection

As I compose myself and open my mind up to allow the flow of this message that is streaming through me for you, I can't help but reflect on how far off I used to be in my own life. Struggle, self-sabotage, low self-esteem, an overdose of insecurity and an overgrown inferiority complex used to be my constant companions. Even once I had the intellectual resources and training in my field, I still held on to a lot of fear and doubt. I was afraid to speak with my own voice and very often spoke only words of my teachers or those that I was told were the wise and successful ones. I couldn't get myself to find my own voice and speak my own experiences and ideas because I thought, "Who would really want to hear what I have to say?" But deep down there was a desire that burned and consumed me to such a great extent that I reached a point where I couldn't be in the shadows of my great mentors no matter how much I loved them. That desire I recognize today as a higher power and intelligence that somehow found its way to me. It is what uses me and gives me the strength to share the words you're reading, so I am certain, as sure as the sun will always rise each morning and bring daylight with it, there is something unknown powering all of us. This is a Source that is invisible to the senses, that cannot be named or even known intellectually—yet it is always connected to us. However, we can and do determine how strong that connection is and I believe social conditioning has made us develop a kind of amnesia that causes us to live life in complete ignorance of this magnificent truth. So while we cannot cut ourselves from it entirely, we can corrode and weaken that connection to such an excessive and devastating extent that we feel like it is no longer there. I think for many of us, especially those who have had a lot of dark times, this is the case.

I know you might be wondering why this is relevant to you in your quest to manifest success and happiness in your life. I want to tell you that although there are numerous approaches I have been taught and discovered by myself on how best to begin to understand the process for creating new results in your life or even your purpose for being here in the first place, none is as simple and enlightening as that of starting from the main Source. This is not to say that other approaches do not work or are wrong. Most are just as good depending on your preference and they all have equal advantages and disadvantages. At the end of the day, each one helps to access that channel or portal to greater wisdom and advancement of the human mind.

In my approach, we begin by shifting your perspective and the starting point for everything you do and think of in your life. I am aware this will stretch you and perhaps challenge you, as it did for me in the beginning because I was very much influenced by my environment of lack, destitution, aggression and victimization. My wonderful well-meaning mother was the only relation I had, and she served as a strong anchor and enhancer for many detrimental beliefs and superstitions that were all based on a model of the world that we both saw. Most of us aren't consciously aware of the fact that we run our lives and view our world based on beliefs, paradigms, concepts and thought patterns that have been passed on to us either genetically or environmentally. This can be a huge obstacle for any individual who doesn't make a conscious effort to create new thought patterns and paradigms. We pick up a lot of things from our parents—especially our mothers—and as women wanting to make it in this new world that we find ourselves in, we will find that using these same methods and ideologies to create the results we want will leave us frustrated, angry, depleted and, in many cases, accompanied by disease and ill health. This is certainly not what I want for you or your loved ones, and regardless of what anyone around you says, it doesn't have to be that way any more. All that you picked up from your mother, who probably picked it up from her mother and so on, doesn't have to be passed on to your children. It can end right now with you. But where do we begin?

The only place we can and must commence from is the place that originates everything we experience as reality. To attempt to fight or end what we can already see, hear, taste, smell and touch through physical action is one of the grave mistakes society continues to make today. There is no way you can create a new result by fighting the existing one because the old simple axiom holds true: whatever you focus your attention upon must grow and expand. This is why Buckminster Fuller's words are not just wise sentiments but scientific facts that apply to everything in life: "You never change things by fighting the existing reality. To change something, build a new model that makes the old model obsolete."

In your world this means that it's about time to put down the weapons of destruction that you've been using in an attempt to change what you don't like and start the process of creation. In truth, you never really create anything because creation is already done, but you are the one who must line up in accordance with the fundamental principles that will bring what you wish to have into your experience. In other words, the starting point must be counterintuitive to what the masses have come to believe. Many people only know themselves to be a physical thing in a physical universe. Typical schooling does not help because it only teaches and emphasizes the physical senses and the physical world. But this manifested world did not create itself, for we now know from the brilliant work of the scientists that particles do not produce more particles. The field of quantum physics—though relatively new—has completely revolutionized science and the universe as a whole. For many years we believed that the tiniest particle was the originating substance for everything, including you and I. Now we know that once broken down, even the tiniest matter (quarks), turns into non-matter: a quantum field of potential energy that is non-local and non-empirical. What a relief for humankind and what a gift it has been that we are smart enough to discover that we all have the power and potential to be, do and have anything we want as long as we tap into that field of potentiality.

It is a great time for all of us to be alive, and you are at the frontline of this discovery as a modern woman alive today because you get to demonstrate the power that you have to rewrite your own destiny. It cannot come from protesting against what has already been materialized, but it must be from that original non-empirical field of potentiality as scientists call it, or Energy, or Source, or God—or whatever you feel inclined to refer to it as. As I said, it is untouchable, completely invisible to the senses and cannot be named. Therefore it is not the name that matters but the knowing of it. This is the very substance or Source that I was referring to at the beginning of this chapter and it is the only one I will continue to reference throughout this book as Spirit/God/ Source/ Energy/Prime Creator because I know with all that I am, it is all there really is.

If you begin to take on the perspective that everything is fundamentally energy and that you are made of this same originating substance, life begins to take on a new meaning because rather than feeling like a victim of life you recognize that you are the master of it (with a serious case of amnesia!). There is a famous line I once heard that I love which says that we are rich millionaires who live like beggars because we have forgotten who we are and what we have. I want to invite you to claim your riches by remembering who you are and what you have but the first and most important ingredient to aid you in this revelation and realization must be that which will enable the renewal of your mind. For it is your mind that directs, governs and regulates what you'll manifest as reality. Without a renewal of your mind, nothing new will manifest in your life no matter how many books, seminars and trainings you get. This is why the main ingredient you must add into your world starting now is a strong burning Desire.

Desire

There are many who have been led to believe that desire is bad or unspiritual in some way, but this is just one of those old myths that needs to be discarded. The contrary holds true in fact. Your desire is Spirit seeking to express itself through you and as you. It is a seed planted within you, and this is why many times a true desire always appears impossible to the rational or ego mind because physically there are no signs of its actualization or practicality.

I have always had a strong liking and connection with butterflies for some reason. My personality tends to be quite similar to the carefree nature of the butterfly in many aspects and it causes me to be quite misunderstood—especially by those who would prefer I fit into their ideas of life. But if you observe the caterpillar, there is nothing about it that demonstrates the manifestation of the butterfly. Absolutely nothing! From a physical point of view it seems impossible that a caterpillar can ever become a butterfly and yet it does. The desire and intention that remains seeded within is all that it needs to make it a reality.

The same is true for you when it comes to your desires, and this is why you must take the time to discover what is your truest, deepest desire. That which you want more than anything else will always lead you into your greatest most fulfilled version of Self and change not just U but the entire Universe as well. There is a gift that only you hold and it isn't from some kind of error but by divine grace that you are the carrier of this gift. As you discover, shine and share this gift, the whole world benefits greatly, no matter how big or small it may appear to you. Anything less than living from that place of greatness will always leave you feeling as you might be feeling now. The path to you being a more bold, beautiful and blissful version of yourself can only be that which enables you to know what you truly desire and then allows that desire to be your bright star to guide you on your path and destiny. It is this desire that will give you all that you need to reconnect, re-establish the relationship you have with Spirit and create the platform by which Spirit can advance and expand in a way that nature would otherwise not spontaneously manage to manifest without you. That is how much of a big deal you are in this Universe.

All that remains now is to ask yourself the simple question:

What do I really really, really want? What is my greatest dream /desire? What do I love?

I invite you to take a moment or two right now and give yourself the space to hear what answers come up for you. Don't skip over this and if possible write down whatever shows up for you. There is an exercise we always do in my coaching which helps any individual really hone down this answer and I have included it at the end of this chapter. I encourage you to play along and participate. Show up for yourself for once if you want life to start showing up for you too.

This particular exercise is so crucial to the success of your journey and it must be done properly. This means that you must listen in for the desire you really want. It won't appear as a result of rational thinking or giving consideration to what others want for you or what you think is possible. The seed you want to find and cultivate is one that you can feel is so mighty, brilliant and humbling there is no way it belongs to your rational mind. That is the seed that is seeking to establish and grow you. Once you know what you really want and desire, connect with it. Indulge in it as a child would and trust that who you really are and what you are capable of is far greater than what you have now.

Of course with that acknowledgement, it becomes natural to wonder: "Well, who am I really? And what gives me this strength and trust? What is this unknown that I should love and surrender to rather than fear?" For that to be understood from our human standpoint, we must gain a better understanding of the body, mind and spirit.

The DESIRE workout

There are four domains in life that we all wish to thrive in: health, relationships, creative expression and financial supply. Now is the best time to give yourself permission to consider what is possible for you. Many people aren't really sure of what their deepest desire is or they limit it to just one thing. I want to invite you to dream big and see where those ideas will take you. So take a moment to describe how you would really love these four areas to manifest in your life. Let your imagination be the commander here and just allow everything to flow no matter how impossible it may seem.

Health	
Relationship	
Creative Expression	
Financial Supply	

Staying in our comfort zone holds us back from experiencing life and fulfilling our desires. For example, we've all been given beliefs about having the right education, income and body image and so we relentlessly pursue these predefined labeled perceptions of success. Some of these conditioned beliefs are hard wired into us at a very early age and others are acquired throughout our formational years by peers and media.

What common behaviors, activities and thoughts have you experienced and seen in your community of peers and family that perhaps you now question as limiting or not in harmony with your passions? List three.

1.

2.

3.

Let's finish this workout by listing 5 things you would love to do if location, age, gender, time, money, education and experience were not factors.

1.

2.

3.

4.

5.

CHAPTER 8

The First Essential (Part II):
Getting into the Spirit of U

The Relationship: Body Mind & Spirit

I believe that the single most important question every individual must ask themselves and live by to make sense of life is, "Who or what am I?" It doesn't matter how young or old you may think yourself to be, or even how satisfied you are with life right now, unless you live this question every day of your life, it will always feel like something is amiss. As a classic example of a lost and angry child suffering from a chronic identity crisis, I wasn't able to find peace no matter where I travelled to or whom I was with until I began living this question. I think I have pretty much made peace an integral part of my life today and that question is still one I strive to gain a deeper answer to. But I am certainly content with what I've been able to discover so far about who I am. This book, however, is about you... so, who are you really?

How much airtime have you given to that single question in your life? I know that especially as women we are so attuned to defining ourselves as daughters, mothers and wives that we probably have a harder time opening ourselves up to that question. I want to invite you to really ponder it personally and allow yourself to be in your own sacred space now, vulnerable enough to hear what comes up. Naturally, for the majority of people, the answer will be based on status, accolades, financial prosperity or some kind of physical accomplishment that one feels defined by. At best, maybe some will say they are their bodies or their brains. But if you define yourself by what you do, have or what you've accomplished, then what happens when these things (as they always do), change or come to an end?

We see a civilization with increasing depression, dissatisfaction, disease and disintegration mainly because most of us have been consumed by a lie! That's right. The things we were told we are in many cases are completely false, yet we bought into this blindly. So as what we think we are changes, it's only natural that we fall into despair and get sucked into a deep hole, because at the end of the day no one wants to lose who they believe themselves to be. This is why death is the biggest fear on most people's list. Why? Because when you move from defining yourself by what you have or do, then your body becomes the next typical focus. But we all know the body is mortal, so it's only natural that dying is a huge deal. Scientists today have revealed to us some astonishing truths that were shared by philosophers, spiritual teachers and seers for thousands of years, yet only recently have we been able to claim these as scientific truth. We know today that your marvelous body and brain are not the ones in charge of creating life or results. These are simply a dynamic manifested plastic ship, so to speak, with a highly intelligent and ever evolving dynamic captain. The commander in charge of this ship is perfectly orchestrating the body through the other miraculous gift we have called the mind, yet is nowhere to be found. Meaning, we can go inside your body and your brain (neuroscientists do this all the time), and we can physically see all the awesome communication, connection and processing that is going inside you, but we cannot figure out where "you" are. Isn't that just incredible? We can study the command center and observe the commands being carried out, but the commander cannot be found in the command center. This being the case, suffice it to say, you must gain a new awareness of who you are because if you still think you are your body, brain or even your mind, you're bound by false invisible chains from the past. Your body and your mind are exactly that: yours. So then, who are you?

For centuries we were led to believe more in separation than oneness. Whether it was between science and religion, between races or gender or between the physical or material world and the non-physical or spiritual world, there was separation everywhere. Things have changed and the world has awakened to a new dawn where we realize that was an error on our part because in the perception of separation and conflict, we moved further away from the ultimate truth and reality. This was a big one for me to get, especially because I have never been spiritual or religious. If anything, I am a material girl and I enjoy physical manifestations a lot! So if you wonder whether I am trying to preach to you or get you to join some kind of organization or religion—I am totally not! What I am aiming to do is get you to seek your answers with a new approach and from a new place that you perhaps never thought of. If you are anything like me, you really never thought of it for sure!

The only path you can walk now that will lead you right into your desired life comes from learning the relationship between your body, mind and Spirit. Why? Because they are different aspects of one and the same that forms the whole: You.

Your body, though magnificent and made up of trillions of cells all working in perfect harmony to ensure that you enjoy maximum comfort and pleasure, is but the effect of a greater underlying cause. Under a microscope, your body is a glistening gleaming radiating form and it is not solid. It's a mass of energy at an astounding speed of vibration and I like to think of it as the material medium and instrument of the mind. This is the house you live in and today's neuroscience has shown us that this house we inhabit is plastic and dynamic in more ways than I have time to detail in this particular book. The take home point for you regarding your body is that, it is indeed a masterpiece—but not the master. This is why I referred to it as the instrument or even the manifestation of something far greater and more miraculous and for the most part completely mysterious to even the most avid scientist in the world: your mind.

Your Mind is beyond miraculous in my eyes. It is definitely my biggest passion to study, understand and master my mind and what I have learned along the way is that the more I understand my mind, the more I understand yours because there is only one mind. While science still has very little knowledge of the full functions and capabilities of the mind, I think it's safe to say that from what we know from science, philosophy and theology, that the mind has infinite potential that is, for the most, part unknown to humankind. Even with all the advancement and technology we have today, we are still infants in our knowledge of what the mind is capable of. I want to make life easier for you by simplifying the boring, formal and many times complicated concepts about the mind which probably make most people shut down and want to watch TV instead. So, I will talk street talk about the mind to give you simple and vital ideas that you must begin to play with that will aid you in understanding why you must develop your mind and become the master of it if you want lasting change.

Let's define the mind in simple terms

The best definition I have found after being fortunate enough to be trained by some of the best experts on this topic is that your mind is an embodied and relational process that regulates the flow of energy and information. Translation: Mind is movement and it is not your brain.

Your mind is in every cell, organ and atom of your body. It is everywhere and is everything you call your body. Since Einstein changed the history of science when he discovered the most famous equation ($E=MC^2$ which basically means everything is energy) it becomes essential to direct and regulate your mind appropriately because it is here that the flow and exchange of energy and information is regulated and directed. This is the level where the energy of your life takes form. To know and master your mind is to master life and guarantee yourself a life beyond your wildest imagination.

This is why the most essential step for you to make is to realize that you have a body which is the material instrument through which your mind is manifesting itself. The mind—which is the connecting bridge and director of the form and shape that your body and your physical world will take—is still not who you really are. It is the conduit between the True non-physical "you" and the formed physical "you" reading this now. So here we get to a very interesting juncture, because we are completely stepping out of the physical or material realm and into a reality taught by very few and practiced by even fewer. This is the world of Cause. It is where everything begins, believe it or not, and it's the starting point that you need to place yourself in mentally to manifest a new, more authentic, bold and prosperous version of you. Your mind and how developed it currently is might be the only obstacle on your way. This often is the case for the majority of people, so please don't worry. Focus and understanding is key here because to raise your level of awareness and strengthen this bridge in a manner that serves you and sets you up for success is the only work for you today. Your success has very little to do with the current circumstances and conditions in your life and everything to do with your state of being and mental attitude.

Life is a psychological mind game because only from the mind remaining below does duality exist. From the mind moving higher and above to the land of the unknowable and infinite eternalness or Spirit, there is only wholeness. The major problem that we have as a civilization today is that the link that connects the domain of Spirit and that of material is so weak and under developed that it feels unreal. Yet it is the only way we can take our power back. Your mind is the miracle that shapes your world and what you experience as reality, and it has the capacity to create both heaven and hell for you depending on the beliefs and paradigms held within it. So while we don't entirely know what the mind can do, we know some aspects of it and how results are created. What we know without a doubt is that the beliefs and paradigms held by the individual determine pretty much the limitations of the individual. You have the power to think and originate thoughts and you're blessed with higher faculties that very few know about and even fewer utilize effectively. These mental faculties—if specifically and properly developed—guarantee your success because that's just how awesome you are, regardless of your background, location or ethnicity. But nothing is possible if your beliefs do not support your endeavor. So basically think of it like this: the myths, beliefs and ideas you hold about who you are and what you're capable of are literally held within your mind. And they become the emblem that cradles whatever subject you are dealing with, encapsulating it into a problem. Anything beyond that cannot become your reality because the mind will never manifest that which it doesn't believe to be true of itself. This is the beauty of being the highest form of creation on the planet because no other living creature has this ability. So, begin to see your mind metaphorically as a pipe, and imagine that this pipe is connected to a Source that is infinite and powerful. Rewriting your destiny and creating a life you absolutely love—stepping out as a bold, beautiful and blissful woman of today— is not just wishful thinking. It is your birthright because you have the power that creates the world connected to you. How else do you think you are breathing and having your heart beat in perfect harmony even while you sleep? You've got it! Your mind (your pipe) will help bring anything you want from the non-physical into the physical. The question is, how corroded is this pipe? Is it full of rust and substances that cause a blockage of the natural and full flow of this power? Can you see now why you do have the power right where you are to turn your life around and bring forth what the world has never seen before? I certainly hope so…

And all of this wouldn't be possible if you didn't emanate from a Source, one that powers your life. I believe that Source/Spirit/ Energy, is who you are. It is the real you, the sacred powerful and whole you that is sitting behind all these wonders we have been talking about. That Spirit or sacred-Self is the commander and I know that with everything I am. But words don't teach, I can only hope that you will take the words and live them out in your life and let life show you this knowledge through experience. If you pause for a moment now and reflect on this relationship we have established and connected that began with the well known physical domain (which I call effects) and ended with the untouchable, un-nameable non-physical domain (which I call the cause), doesn't it make sense to you now that your only requisite is to begin your planning, your point of creation for any desire at the root Cause?

Your desire is always going to be as far out of reach or as near as you allow it to be. It is only through your mind, through the cleansing, developing and strengthening of your pipe that you will open the floodgates and allow heaven on earth to manifest for you. There must be a connection and relationship in an orderly and harmonious way if you truly want to become a powerful manifester. Where you stand now is so irrelevant to the Source and power that is always there for you because it is you! When will you wake up and find your Self, take advantage of this information, follow your clues, cleanse the pipe and realize your dreams? That is completely up to you.

CHAPTER 9

The Second Essential:
Awakening Your "Genie in a Bottle!!"

I recently read a mythical story from Germany about a genie who was trapped in a bottle for eons in the back of a famous museum in Berlin. It's quite a funny educational story and as the teaching goes, all the many adults who walked by the strange looking vessel that housed this genie couldn't hear or even become aware of the genie inside because he spoke a language very different from what we are accustomed to. Even on the rare occasion that some adult from the "outside world" would be intuitively directed to pick up the gorgeous and mysterious looking bottle, the genie in all his attempts couldn't manage to get their attention long enough to make himself known. This went on until one day a child happened to get lost and found himself in this part of the museum (which rarely happened) and upon spotting this bottle immediately followed his natural instinct to play with it. He started talking to it, tried popping it open and peeping inside, curious about its contents. Upon further examination of this unusual vessel he heard a voice shouting, "I am here"! He was perplexed and almost dropped the bottle. He tried shouting for any adult to come over and see this talking bottle, but because he was lost in the back, no one responded immediately. The genie was dazzled by the fact that finally someone in the outside world could understand him and he was overjoyed that he had finally made contact. He explained to the child how to rub the bottle the right way to allow him to emerge, and as the story goes, the genie lived happily ever after serving and protecting the boy, who naturally had all his wishes fulfilled.

I know you might laugh at the simplicity of this fable or even the more famed one of Aladdin and his magic lamp that gave him everything he desired in life, but like them, you pretty much own your very own genie in a bottle. And perhaps like in the story, aren't benefiting much because your conscious connection and communication is almost non-existent. The genie I am referring to is to be found at the quantum level. I believe the mind is the most precious gift in all of creation for humankind and an absolute miracle. Being the medium Spirit uses to navigate this earth and manifest itself into a physical thing, your mind is literally what manifests what you consider reality. It can do so by design as I am about to show you or by default through past thinking patterns and inherited belief systems.

The full functionality of your mind still remains a mystery to all of humankind but there are certain aspects that science has helped us understand now. I will share with you the process by which you create your reality and results and how you can begin to "rub your genie bottle" the right way so you can strengthen and enhance that line of connection and communication in your world. What many of us aren't aware of is the fact that we think in pictures. If I ask you now to think of your favorite holiday destination, your mum or dad, your spouse or if I call out the name of your child, what springs up on the screen of your mind? Not lettered words but images. Pictures of the words and ideas I suggested. You can go into any sacred or ancient script, religious or philosophical, and you will find this illustrated there as well. Though I am not religious, I am aware of religious writings like the Bible where the book of Genesis speaks about the beginning of creation where God or the Source of all creation is said to have commanded the formation of heaven and earth. But he didn't just use vague words—he specifically used clear precise images whether they were fruits, flowers, animals and so on. He turned the formless into form through imagery. This idea is crucial for your growth and transformation and should be fully internalized in your mind because you have the same power to bring forth from the formless whatever you desire. As a matter of fact, you have already been doing this, perhaps more on default than anything, which has caused you more agony than happiness. But once you learn how to call upon your genie by rubbing the bottle the right way so it will manifest your commands, you will turn your life story into an epic one. You have an opportunity to use your mind to form clear images that will come to pass if in accordance with the Law of life.

Rubbing the Bottle With the Genie the Right Way

Now that we get that we think in pictures only, it's imperative that we think only of the pictures we desire to materialize. Your mind has no sense of humor, my dear reader, and the sooner you get that, the faster you will re-create your life and everything that's of value to you. There are two elements that play a big role in the manifestation of your results and while they are equally important—albeit, handling different roles—the harmonious alignment of the two and correlation with what I call the parent mind (also known as the super conscious mind) is the primary work for you to master in order to live your best life yet. As you gain mastery of your mind, the game of life becomes child's play. So the first part that we want to shine some light on is your conscious mind. This is your starting point for any new creation that you would like to experience in your world.

Humankind is made in the image and likeness of God and success is every individual's birthright. Although quite a number of people have heard some version of that statement, very few actually understand what it means. Surely it can't mean our physical body—we are all so different with extremely diverse features, colours, shapes and sizes. Quite frankly, I despised that statement for most of my life because the God of my upbringing was unjust and capricious. I figured he must look like those who were educated, rich and successful, but definitely not like my family or I. The biggest error we continue to make while we advance as a human race is making God in our own image and thus creating the chaos, separation and hatred that seems to be growing globally. When we refrain from making God into a human image and retrain ourselves into understanding what that statement really means, not only will people respect and love each other's differences but I believe miracles will become the order of the day in such an environment. So you and I truly are made in the image and likeness of the originating Source and that image and likeness does not refer to the physical bodies we manifest, but the formless thinking intelligence by which we make manifest the expression, experience and quality of what we call life. In other words, I am not saying that you can stop creation from happening—your life is going to keep creating and happening until your last breath. But you do have choice over the kind of experiences and manifestations that you will have. In order to realize this as a practical reality, it's essential that you make as your starting point anything you wish to be, do, have, create and experience in this world as your conscious mind.

However, be forewarned that your conscious mind is also the aspect of you that connects you to your external surroundings and enables you to communicate and comprehend. What do I mean by this? You have linked to your conscious mind the physical senses that we are well accustomed to. School, society, our community and parents promote the use of the five physical senses literally from the moment we pop into this world. So you are a master at relying on your senses to navigate this world and while seeing, tasting, touching, hearing and smelling are important, they are not the manner by which you can exercise your creative abilities to design your life or even learn how to rub your bottle with the genie the right way. This is why most people have the sequence for creating new results backwards and end up having to struggle so much just to reach their desired goals. The five physical senses are beautiful but they are always condition based and limited to navigating and tapping into what is already made manifest. The process of deliberate creation requires the God-given faculties and gifts hidden within your mind that we are never taught about and thus never develop. So for many of us these are like unused muscles; you can imagine going through life never strengthening your muscles and then wondering why your body is so frail. Should you choose to have strong muscles and a toned healthy looking body, you know it would take some changes and a shift in perspective. For example, you would start exercising and developing those muscles gradually until they finally grow and begin to serve you. The same is true for your mental faculties. In my other materials and books I go through each of the faculties in greater detail and I strongly recommend that you make the decision to find out more about your higher faculties and how you can strengthen and develop them. They are named as: Intuition, Imagination, Perception, Will, Memory and Reasoning. Though they are all very powerful and important for designing the quality of the life you would love to experience, I believe that perception, imagination and intuition are the primary and most vital ones to develop for anyone who is hungry for fast results. I have devoted an entire training course to imagination because I feel so strongly about the power behind grasping and learning how to control your imaginative power. Even Einstein is known to have said that imagination is the only thing more important than knowledge, so clearly there is great power in enhancing your imagination. In this journey you are on of becoming a thriving modern woman who is not only bold and beautiful but extremely blissful, imagination is a faculty you must nail down.

Hence the conscious mind is where all the intellectual processes and initial designing of your life happens. It is through right thought that you begin molding your new life in the conscious mind with the help of your higher faculties. As you can see, there is a creative thinking process that needs to take place, one that is inspired in the mind of the individual independent of current conditions and circumstances. This ability to think what you want to think regardless of circumstances is the same faculty that God used in the book of Genesis, for nothing in that formless void exhibited any sign of what he then created. If we consider what today's scientists tell us about matter, the same concept would apply because quantum mechanics state that before an observation is made by an observer, there are both waves and particles existing simultaneously and in every case, every thing can be fundamentally reduced to an energy field that is non-local, which is what gives rise to particles. It is therefore your mind, given to you by the ultimate creator, that makes you the highest form of creation and a co-creator in this universe made in the likeness of that which makes everything. I believe you are starting to see just how powerful and extraordinary you are. Your conscious mind is the only place you need to go to start the wheels of your success rolling in a new direction and establish yourself as the woman you intend to become.

The next aspect of your mind we will consider is your sub-conscious mind. Here I wish to bring to your attention the noted difference in the role it plays when it comes to manifesting in your material world. While the conscious mind is capable of discerning difference and choosing whether to accept or reject any information or idea presented, the sub-conscious mind is completely deductive and accepts everything as good. This is the part of the mind your emotions call home and we also know that it is the part of you that has direct contact with universal intelligence or the super-conscious parent mind. This means that it is not only unlimited in power but pretty much determines what will finally materialize in your physical world. How? Based on the stored information that it holds as beliefs, habits and the gathered image you have of yourself. We use a generic word for all of these: paradigms. This is where it gets even more intriguing for those of us who love to study the mind. The invisible laws that govern your wellbeing and success do not understand the intellectual aspect of your mind where language, rational thinking and similar things go on, but rather they understand and consistently respond to the emotional, vibrational aspect of your mind. In other words, the language of the universe isn't what you grew up speaking, it is this emotional, vibrational communication. Your emotions are determined by the beliefs, meanings, definitions and paradigms that you have stored in your mind. Most of this was deposited there before you could even think for yourself! And what's even crazier is that you spend most of your waking hours running from your sub-conscious mind, which will then determine your behavior and the actions you take and thus the results you can manifest. So if you grew up with paradigms of lack, limitation and insecurity or not enough, can you see why all the physical effort to have it all in life and live a life different from what you have is going to be in vain or just drain away all your energy?

Many women today are barely making it to the end of the day and once home it's just more drama with kids who are uncontrollable and never listen, a husband who's never home or supportive enough and a body that they feel ashamed of. When was the last time you stood naked in front of a mirror and just fell in love with everything you saw? Well, how can you if all your life the images of girls who looked nothing like you became the symbol you stored in your mind as the definition of beauty? See how this works!

Although it might seem hard or awkward in the beginning to park the idea in you mind that what you think, how you feel and what manifests in your world are very much related, I hope you can at least not reject it for now. I am not asking that you believe me but I am asking you to consider the possibility and then test it out for yourself so you can know for sure. In any case, most everything you think and believe to be true was accumulated in your DNA before birth and then through your parents, school, media and environment since birth. Unless you are part of the minority of individuals who either came from awesome backgrounds with thriving paradigms or you've been a student of self-awareness for a while, chances are, just as I had to do, you have to clean up and reboot your thinking and storage system. You need to cleanse that mind, develop it, strengthen it and reconnect with the powerful Source that already contains the life you've been dreaming of.

CHAPTER 10

The Third Essential:
Re-Defining, Rewriting and Revamping U

As I sit to write this chapter for you, consumed by the charismatic calmness and magnificence of the sea view in my home, I can't help but feel that there is much we can learn just by slowing down enough to appreciate and observe nature. If I look around me I see the beauty and finesse by which nature operates as the sun begins to rise and day breaks. The breathtaking and colourful performance that the sun performs with the sky at every sunrise and sunset remains unmatched and the reflection of all this glory on the surface of the sea, which is constantly moving and flowing, reminds me how imperative it is for us to be flexible and constantly renewing ourselves because change is the only constant in this world. To think that change only happens periodically and is somewhat a bad thing is the beginning of all frustration. Change is inevitable and it is the only constant in nature. That should tell us a lot already, because it means that real progress, true love, beauty, happiness and our own paradigms must be flexible enough to accommodate and transcend change. However, most of us believe the contrary. The average woman has a very hard time adapting and being flexible or even initiating something new in her life. We are a society that lives off mass thinking, social conditioning and habits. We have settled into a comfort zone type of lifestyle and trust rigidly in our routines no matter how good or bad they are. I am not saying that we shouldn't have a strategy or guidelines for how we live life on a daily basis but I am insisting that we incorporate a lot more flexibility and flair into our daily rituals.

A homemaker will almost always dress the same, take the same road, cook the same food, think the same thoughts, have the same fights and expect the same things every single day. The same goes for the corporate world working woman or entrepreneur. If we track the thinking patterns of these different personality types, it won't be too hard to figure out why they have what they've got and why they're not getting something new. To get something new in your life you must start being and doing something different from what you've been doing so far. That's why Einstein said his definition of insanity is doing the same thing over and over again and expecting new results! It just won't happen. If you are taking the time and effort to read this book because you wish to manifest something new in your life and you want to design a new lifestyle for yourself where you have it all on your terms and you feel authentically powerful, beautiful and in total bliss, you must stop repeating what you've been doing so far that clearly doesn't work well enough to get you where you want to be. You need to be willing to pause and start asking with a new attitude for the new solution that you seek because where you're at now is at the level of the problem and you may wish all you want to become that better version of yourself, but it's never going to happen no matter how much struggle or effort you put in. You know why? The solution cannot and will not be found at the same level as the problem—ever! And it doesn't matter if you are seeking to manifest in the area of finances, personal or professional relationships, health and wellbeing, spiritual or material—the principles are still the same. You must gain your new starting point and make a serious decision and commitment to yourself that this is your time and you've got what it takes to build your dream life. Then start adapting to a renewal of your mind and allow yourself to be flexible and curious enough to welcome in new things, ideas and experiences: the unknown. I call this revamping and reinventing yourself.

If you are a mother who has a routine that you follow every day, try something new regularly—even something as simple as rearranging the manner by which you do your everyday chores or the road you use to go pick the kids up from school. The same goes for working women. Make it a priority in your life to try something new as often as you can with your physical body. Whether it's something big like a total makeover, learning a new skill, "girl time", or something small like taking a meditative walk in the park alone or joining that dance or yoga class that you always felt too ashamed to try, all these simple things that we tend to consider unimportant go a long way in nurturing and caring for ourselves. This keeps us fresh and vibrant. Many women today have given up on everything, including their own self-nurturing, and that is one of the pitfalls when wanting to create a life you love. You must be in love with yourself and your life before good things can gravitate to your experience and you need to find ways to keep reinventing yourself on the outside no matter how small. Even more essential is to renew and reinvent what's going on in your inner world. As a matter of fact, until the inner world is revamped, nothing on the outer world will satisfy you and bring you bliss no matter how good it looks. The idea that beauty is only skin deep is something I abhor and totally disagree with. I feel that whoever came up with that conclusion shows a heightened level of ignorance and a lack of understanding of what beauty really is. Beauty is truth and is as real as life itself. There is a huge difference between looking good or fabricating that essence of beauty and being beautiful. The former is temporary and materially centered while the latter is a fundamental truth and expression of Spirit, thus it is eternal and radiant. Each and every one of us is beautiful and I have never seen a baby that isn't born breathtakingly beautiful. The expression of the beauty is what can be masked by social conditioning and thus become clouded, but beauty in its essence is present in all of us, especially you.

Women naturally want to be and feel beautiful because it's in their nature, and rightfully so. The only reason why most struggle with authentically feeling beautiful is because they have an *Outside- in* approach, which is backwards. What we are here to do and then share with others is to learn the truth behind manifesting beauty, bliss and wellbeing in our own lives first, then spread it across our circles of influence. To do this, there are two very powerful tools you have been gifted with which will empower you to make your transformation effective and help you not only redefine who you now want to become but set you up on that path to success as well.

Attention & Intention

I can hardly emphasize enough in words just how dramatically different your world would become if you effectively learned how to use these two powerful gifts. Your focused attention on anything, be it wanted or unwanted, will always bring more of it into your experience. Think about a time when you had thoughts of something that you really didn't want to happen. Maybe you got stuck in traffic and kept worrying you'd be late or you felt insecure about your partner and suspected he was cheating on you only to prove yourself right! Or maybe you kept worrying about being broke and it played itself out just as you had worried it would. These aren't just random consequences, but a lawful result that came about because of the way you were using the power of your focus and attention. There are universal laws that are immutable and non-negotiable. They are always at play and deliver the part of creation that you'll get to experience based upon your choices. The attention you give any subject in your life and the meaning you attach to that attention will always yield a result. Furthermore, the intention you place behind anything is such a powerful force in propelling and ensuring the manifestation itself, that it becomes logical at this point to say you will always get in life what you expect. There is nothing that comes to you that you didn't expect at some level of your being and if you can be candid enough with yourself and just put this idea to the test you will see exactly what I mean. Now, I am not saying that you expect sickness or a cheating spouse or children who don't listen to you or a boss who doesn't appreciate you, but I am saying you might manifest that if you have stored in your sub-conscious mind a tarnished self image that believes you aren't good enough, pretty enough, educated enough, that people take advantage of your goodness or that you could get certain ailments and diseases based on the fact that your parents had it and so on. All these are just few examples of some of the patterns we have stored as expectations that will keep playing out in our world in some way, form or shape. If you were conditioned into believing that life is supposed to be hard or things don't easily go well for you, or good relationships are hard to find, then your expectation must find a way to play itself out in your life in a manner that supports your beliefs and paradigms. What you assume and expect must come to you by law.

Taking control of your focus and directing your attention and intention more consciously and deliberately could literally change your life experiences beyond your greatest imagination. You already have these two gifts now, the only thing you need to know is how to utilize them in service of your dreams and goals rather than against them as you've probably been doing so far. The big idea that I promote is that there is a science of living and you create your own reality guided consciously or unconsciously by this science of life. This is not just a cool hypothesis. It is a proven truth that I didn't even invent. Your attention and the intention behind your daily actions, the thoughts you predominantly hold and the dreams and goals you carry in your heart could literally turn life on earth into heaven or hell for you – that's how powerful you are.

As you become more proficient and masterful in utilizing the power of your attention and intention for the realization of the dreams you wish to manifest, things may not always feel so smooth. Stepping into the unknown requires great strength and courage but it also calls for large doses of enthusiasm, encouragement, excitement and positive expectation. I call these the 4 E's of mastering the art of thriving. The world in general has a deficit of love and we have become a civilization threatened into extinction because of the manner in which we treat each other and our beautiful planet. If there is something that has dropped away in society, it is optimism and a zest for life. Genuine kindness and compassion has become so rare in our interactions that embarking on new challenges can only feel like torture because the average individual has forgotten how it feels to bathe in love and compassion. Many people struggle to reach their goals even when they have the right resources, information, support team and great ideas because they are missing the most important fuels for wellbeing and prosperity. That good feeling has become so rare and in high demand that any artificially manufactured product that promises to produce a "good feeling" becomes an overnight sensation. However good the product may be, the effects cannot be permanent or even long lasting because it still defies your very nature. A zest for life and vitality in everything you do cannot come *to* you but *through* you and *from* you. Until you can cultivate within yourself that good feeling, everything you attempt externally will be at best a short-lived illusion, or at worst, your new addiction. I believe this is why most are convinced that success is a struggle. But it doesn't have to be your story any more because you can apply the 4 E's to anything and everything right now and watch the magic that begins to transpire.

Enthusiasm

H. W. Arnold said that the worst bankruptcy in the world is the person who has lost enthusiasm, and he was right. Many women today have lost all enthusiasm for themselves, for life, for love. It is essential that you bring back high levels of enthusiasm starting now in whatever way you feel possible because without it, nothing great will be achieved by you. With enthusiasm in high gear, you will become unstoppable and inspiring to others. It is the fuel that your dream is waiting for.

Encouragement

When I refer to encouragement, I don't mean looking for encouragement from others. I mean how you talk with/to yourself. Give yourself a pat on the back, chill out a bit more, talk yourself into a more empowered, good feeling place, buy yourself some flowers or chocolate whenever you accomplish something—don't wait for anyone to do for you what you can do for yourself. Teach yourself how to show up for yourself instead of waiting for another to do so. As you show up more for yourself and make your inner world a priority, life will also show up for you. The only opinion that needs to matter in your world should be the one conjured up in your head. The best thing about learning to be the greatest encourager and comforter in your own life is the increased self-confidence, high self-esteem and a strong faith in yourself that will ensue.

Excitement

This is the juice of it all… I get excited and revved up just thinking of how good it feels to be excited! If something doesn't excite you then you are not living on purpose or expressing your best version, period. Many who hear me say this would like to stone me because they feel that life can't possibly be exciting all the time but I don't really care whether the majority agrees with me. I care that you agree that it's important to be excited every single day. Again, let's think about children—they are always excited about everything, even things that seem ordinary and mundane like a game of hide and seek. Where is the magic in that? Yet it's always magic being engaged with a bunch of kids playing hide and seek. You need to recall that same spirit and make your life more exciting to you. It doesn't mean you will be shrieking and bursting out in loud excitement every moment; there's a time to be loudly excited and a time to be in quiet excitement. But in every case there needs to be that spark, and you will know it when you get it. There is no way you can be living or pursing your dreams and desires and not be excited about it. I don't just mean once in a while, I mean your heart should always be singing whenever you are thinking or engaging in the building and designing of your life. If that's not happening then just as a student learning mathematics would work on the equation by applying the laws of math and the formula accurately until they get the correct answer, so too must you work on the equation of your life and apply the law-based formula of manifestation until you feel good and excited about where you are, where you are going and everything else in between. That is the fastest way to manifest what others would consider magic and miracles.

Expectation

If you nail the first three, this last one will flow naturally just as the river flows to the sea. You will inherently reach your goals and live your utmost life when you positively expect it to be your norm. What very few are aware of is the role of expectation relative to the law of attraction which manages what manifests in your world. There are two phases needed in the attraction process. The first phase is easier to get, and is called desire, and the second phase is expectation. They are actually two sides of the same coin so to speak, because desire summons creative energy while expectation reels it in and directs it into full formation. If the desire is true and magnificent and summons the energy, but there is no expectation to direct it and reel it back to you, then that desire will remain out in the invisible realm for a very long time. You see how this works? Let's use a quick image to cement this further. Imagine you are a fisherman out at sea and you've got your perfect bait and fishing rod. Desire is when you throw in the bait and the fish automatically hooks on the fishing rod. As best said by Jesus Christ, ask and it is given. It is always given to you, but expectation happens when you reel in the rod to bring it up on your boat. Now if you have positive expectations then it's a done deal. You will bring that manifestation to life, but if you have doubts and fears or you want it but don't expect it, then it would be like sitting on that boat with a fish hooked at the end of fishing line but still in the water. You can pray all you want and complain all you want but unless you reel it in, that fish is never ending up in your hands. That's how important expectation is and now you know exactly what to do as you build your dream.

Things are always working out for you all the time and the only reason why you stumble or manifest things that you don't want is because somewhere along the line there was a blockage. If there is nothing blocking you, only your greatest desires will flow to your experience. These blockages are all stored as paradigms and so creating new paradigms, along with applying everything we have discussed so far and drinking in huge doses of the 4 E's is guaranteed to land you in whatever destination you feel is worthy of you.

It is time for you to pick up your dreams and begin employing these ideas in your life. Your destiny belongs to you and as long as it's not being realized by you, the world is missing out and lacking that unique expression and gift that you came here to give and live. I believe that you can now see that rewriting the script of your life is not such a big deal. In fact, it's simpler than all these words I've just used to try and detail for you exactly what it takes. As it turns out, so far, every ingredient, tool or power that you need to create a whole new world for yourself is actually within you now. You don't need to buy anything or pay anyone or even learn anything more. You've already got what it takes to start moving in the direction that will generate more of what you want. Here is the most amazing part: as you step into thriving and becoming a more bold, beautiful and blissful version of U, you will not only be changing the U that you define yourself as, but the U–niverse itself.

CHAPTER 11

The Fourth Essential: Seeding the Right Dreams the Right Way

We have two main objectives in studying this book. The first is to choose the best dream for our best life and then to use that desire as the starting point of our Self-realization and as the reason for experimenting with life by learning and applying the laws that govern wellbeing and success. The second objective is to use that desire as the focal point for summoning the inherent creative energy within that births everything in life. From there we have to figure out the practical steps to take in order to bring forth the full manifestation. After all, without a point of focus and direction with great clarity, we can never be deliberate designers of our reality. Getting the right dream that hits on both objectives is vital.

This fourth essential is going to show you how to achieve just that. I trust that you went through your desire exercise and that you now have a clear image of what you would love to create, have and share in all the different areas that matter to you. Now it becomes necessary to pick the main one that ranks slightly above the others and focus on employing these principles with the deliberate intent of learning how the process of creation works in your life. If you don't have a dream picked out yet for whatever reason, please choose one now. Just make one up, even if in this moment it just sounds ridiculous and impossible. You will see: if you get to keep breathing for the next twelve months, at the end of that time you will have results showing up in your world whether wanted or not .

Creation never stops and you are constantly creating results either by default or by design. So at least let yourself consider the possibility of creating something you would actually love, whether you see it happening or not. You don't have to know how it will happen, you just need to choose something you've always really wanted.

However, before we can take your dream and sow it, let's make sure that you actually have the right one. I have discovered that many women are working with the wrong dream and so they get frustrated with the outcomes. The right desire that is truly what you want can and must manifest when the proper principles are applied and adhered to. If you've experienced disappointment in the past when you invested your time, energy, effort and money chasing after a dream only to have it fail soon after, or if it turned out unsatisfactory in some way or worse still, if it continues to stagnate and elude you after all the hard work, then you know how distraught you can feel about life. I empathize greatly with that because I've been stuck on that endless loop several times.

I have a client who first came to me in utter frustration over her ongoing business that was performing poorly. She was worried that she would have to close down her services in a few months or move to a smaller and less comfortable location. She offers beauty services and has five employees in her establishment. They had been struggling and scraping by for months on end. Finally it became critical. She was at such a tipping point in her professional role that it started taking a toll on her kids and husband. From where she stood, she could not connect the distress and disappointment at work with the increased arguments and irritation in her personal life. "Boys are always misbehaving", she said to me, "and men just aren't supportive enough. It's hard to find a good marriage nowadays and I feel like everyone takes advantage of me at home." How many times have you felt something similar in your life?

Many times we want to separate and categorize things, making them look unrelated, but abundance and wellbeing don't discriminate one aspect from another. Everything in your life flows from the same source and is always correlated. That's why true success is about being holistic and enjoying all areas that are important to you as an individual. In her case, her business was important and so was her family. The lawful way of nature is to find that balance where she could have it all. She is a wonderful, talented and hard working individual, so I was keen to help her redesign her life and business. Upon first inquiry on what she really wanted, I realized she was more aware of what she didn't want than what she wanted! She kept repeating similar statements like, " The economy is bad and women aren't spending as much as they used to so I think I might have to cut down my team and move to a really small space, which I hate." And I would keep asking if that's what she really wanted, which of course, it wasn't. After a few deep consultations she finally declared that she knew what her dream was. Her dream was to downsize her team but remain in the same location. Rather than have the entire space for beauty services, she would convert half of it into a small boutique to sell vintage clothes. Now the idea that she relayed was more detailed. It certainly sounded good to me because beauty and vintage fashion together are favorites for me. But it would not be true to the message I share if I had let her fall into one of those repetitive loops again. You see, although the idea was great, it wasn't her deepest, truest desire. The idea of beauty and vintage fashion in the same location was her choosing what felt possible based on the conditions she was facing and the fact that she had already done something similar in the past.

The result of our working together and getting her to a place where she boldly picked her right dream and reinvented her life in a manner that accommodated the realization of her deepest desire has been progressing rapidly and this lady is on fire! She's revved up her sales and attracted better employees who offer far better services than before. Soon she will launch a new business model to top that. Just from having that zest and excitement for life rekindled within herself, you can imagine how she's showing up in her personal life as well. I am happy to report that she is no longer a woman who believes that happy marriages don't exist.

In just a matter of months she's gone from zero with no hope of living out her true dreams that seemed to be mere fantasy, to a modern day thriving woman full of passion and joy.

I share this story with you because we can learn something really important here. The dream you choose now must be life giving and it must be what you really love. That's why I want to point out to you the major mistake most women are making when choosing their dream and how you can avoid that same error and ensure that your dream not only brings you satisfaction and prosperity, but opens you up to the path of love, bliss and wellbeing. This all comes together when you find your deepest desire. How does one do it? It begins with you learning that there are 3 ways of choosing your dream.

- The first way is choosing the dream that you know you can have because you've already done it in the past. For example, if you say your dream is to own a BMW but you currently own an older version or similar type of car, that's something you already know how to have. It won't meet the two main objectives we laid out at the start of this chapter. The same was true for my client. She was working with this level of dream picking, which is the wrong way to go if you want to unleash your potential.
- The second way is choosing the dream that you think you can have or create because according to the plans, strategy, conditions or connections that you can think of, it seems like a possibility. This is not your path to greatness either. It is your ego-driven mind trying to dominate and run your life. In the end, this path is always grueling and dissatisfying, yielding mediocre results at best. The majority of people settle for this way.
- The third way is choosing the dream that you really, really, really want because you're absolutely in love with it even though you have no idea how to make it happen. It is the path least travelled by most because it requires great courage, strength and faith. It is the path of the individual that turns an ordinary life into something extraordinary. It's what your heart secretly calls for because it wants to shine. It's the fantasy inside your

customized imagination. As you give birth to the idea, your heart comes alive and bursts into song and dance. It's so rich, so amazing, so breathtaking and exciting that when you think about it you have trouble thinking of anything other than this dream. Think of a time when you fell in love and you just couldn't focus on anything else. You'd wake up in the morning and it's like you slept with a hanger in your mouth ☺. That's exactly how your deepest desire will feel for you. Life will have colour again and even though you have no idea "how" to make it happen and all of the manifested evidence around you doesn't yet support the materialization of this dream, know that you have arrived at the starting point of your greatness. This is the seed—the right seed for you to plant. This is the dream you must go for, starting now.

If you feel you've got it, then we only need ask three questions now to test if it is the right and blessed dream that will bring down your heaven here on earth. Please take a moment and test drive the dream you have now chosen to see if it is the key that unlocks your new reality.

1. Does it give you more life? (it must feel life giving to you)
2. Is it benefiting you and others as well?
3. Do you feel that you need or require a higher power or guidance greater than your physical self to turn this dream into practical reality?

Once you have answered "Yes" you are ready to take this seed that is your God-given gift of expressing greatness and sow it in the fertile soil of your mind, where if well cared for and properly nurtured, it must come to pass by law and manifest in the physical world. I have been known to say many times that God is not a coward, therefore it's impossible that he would give you cowardly desires or even support them. That's why only the brave ones at heart who master their mind and live out their dreams in life, shine and unfurl their greatness for all to see and enjoy. Your dream will be nothing short of a miracle because you are nothing short of magic and miracles. This isn't about your place as a woman, wife, mother, daughter or any of those labels that you might use to pull yourself down. This is about you and your destiny. Your dream will take you there and the power that gives you life is eagerly awaiting your initiation. Seed the right dream, take the decision, trust in the power that breathes life in you and then take one last crucial action to guarantee that your desire manifests naturally.

The subtle law of assumption:

One of the few places you will ever find this next concept is in all my teaching materials. Many brilliant coaches and teachers today leave out this crucial aspect of deliberate creation and manifestation. I've had numerous occasions where an attendee in one of my workshops or seminars who already has a coach and understands personal development really well expresses their frustration in the delay of their dreams actualizing. They nailed the information, internalized it fully, surrounded themselves with the right support groups and continue to study and receive coaching guidance, but the dreams are still lingering on the horizon. Can you relate?

I discovered a great secret a while back in the most unconventional places. After hours of deep investigation and research, it all fell into place. I think every successful person knows this law and uses it to their advantage but very few share it simply because it's almost impossible to pin down. I think of it as trying to grasp water with your hand. We all know how futile this is because the only way to experience water in our hands is to let it flow, keeping our hand as natural and flexible as possible. This law is very similar. This might be why it's rarely shared with great precision despite the fact that it is of the essence when learning the role you play in the creative process. I sincerely hope that I can at the very least give you a sense of what you want to begin reaching for in your mind so you can experience its effects materially. This subtle law that Neville Goddard calls the Law of Assumption is silent and always remains in the background, so most people miss it.

As my industry blossoms and the media hype and commercialization increases, this particular understanding remains elusive and unspoken perhaps because even the so-called experts and gurus of today haven't figured out how to share it with others in a practical and helpful way. Thus, we can overdramatize other more glamorous and sexy laws that fit the commercial and sales strategies better, but for the individual who really has a rags story and wishes to thrive despite this bad start, the process of manifestation will still feel mysterious and based on chance or luck. Without a conscious understanding of, and relation to this subtle law, nothing can materialize. Perhaps this is why many people think that success and thriving is dependent on a certain location or country.

If we look at Italians as an example, they strongly believe that there are more opportunities and chances for them to thrive in America than in Italy. Sure enough when they do go to America they very often live out their dream life. As you will see, this is only because of the unconscious use of this very law. Thus, it has been my strong conviction that we can produce individuals and communities of people who are thriving and living their dream lifestyle in any location anywhere in the world as long as there is proper knowledge of the right practices and principles behind dream building and the ability to thrive. That includes you and your dream. This is the work that remains for you to do once you have sown the right dreams in your life. Take on the position of first and foremost being (rather than doing) the desire you are working toward. And in this state of being, what you are aiming to gain first is the feeling or the essence of the dream itself, and bringing it from that future manifested result into your now. In other words, yes, you can begin to take physical action and effort in the direction of your dreams, but only after you have taken up the essence, the feeling of being the one who already has what you desire to manifest. Be that individual that you must become once you are living your dream. This may sound awkward and even appear hard at first especially if your dream is something you've never had and you've got no reference to go by. But it is the only way manifestation occurs. That's why so many people who study personal development still have a hard time generating results. You, however, have a huge advantage from now on because not only do you know how to choose the right dreams, you also know how to go about manifesting them in the right way. The main thing to do first is to be, in order to ensure it's full manifestation. What a glorious day this will be, what a productive week, month and year this will be for you if you accurately apply this single idea in your activities.

To elaborate further: think of the fact that you wish to have more happiness, love, and prosperity in your life. You want to become more confident and bold in your affairs and feel beautiful and blissful. All of this will manifest naturally when you assume that you already are all those qualities. Does it happen instantly? Nope! It might take a while, but relatively speaking, it's not that long and every day, every moment you are able to sustain that assumption and make it as natural as it is for you to breath, you amplify your manifestation. So, from the example I used earlier of Italians who go to America and live their best lives yet had struggled while still in Italy, you can rest assured that the particular individual used the same law. When they got to America, they received their manifestation because they had taken on the assumption that more success is available to them in America than in Italy. When thinking of the essence of their dream it becomes natural for them to be and feel and expect success there and not here. You can never get what you don't expect to come to you: it is law.

Here's another trivial example that demonstrates what I mean when I speak of the Law of Assumption. I am blessed to have a lot of thick healthy hair. Three years ago I was disappointed by the results I was getting with my then hairdresser and I decided in a single moment to cut off my hair and start again. After I had done it, everyone in my life was frantic over what they felt was a dramatic decision. But for me, it was natural that I have lots of strong healthy long hair. So I cut it because I assumed it would naturally come back just the same if not better. My expectation and my assumptions were in alignment and it wasn't forced or faked up. It was as natural to me that I will have a full head of hair as it is for me to breathe. In time I have manifested exactly that! My friends who have weak and scattered hair wouldn't succeed at the same feat because their assumptions and expectations fall into lack and limitation in relation to their hair. Unless that perspective is shifted to one of faith and an assumption that they too can have healthy looking hair, they will have a very hard time manifesting it.

If you think about it, every day you brush your hair and some of it falls off but you never get stressed over that because it's natural to you that more hair is growing. If your assumption should change, your hair will change. This is what I mean when I say this law will propel the manifestation of what you've consented as true and natural to you. That is a huge deal because it means you could very well keep the thing you desire the most out of reach for a long time if you don't assume it naturally belongs to you.

Whether you've been swayed by the hype of the law of attraction or not, I urge you to pay closer attention to this subtle law. It has no name and no fame, yet it plays a crucial role in what manifests for you. The great teachers and seers left it unnamed and the few who did name it opted to call it the Law of Assumption, which is what I will stick to as well. Seed the right dreams for yourself and take on the assumption of being the one who already is and has what you are desiring to manifest and life will be far beyond your greatest imagination – it's Law.

CHAPTER 12

The Fifth Essential: The Simple Formula and A New Workout Routine

In many of my lectures I share part of my story and how puzzled I was by the fact that in the same country where I grew up in poverty, others were thriving and living at the same level as those in a First World country. In fact, along my climb to success I remember sitting in my townhouse bedroom one morning admiring the walk-in closet I had and the amount of space that I called my bedroom. Then I thought about the fact that at one point I was living in a wooden house the size of my walk-in closet, yet my family and I had to fit in and squeeze ourselves into that. At that moment I was overcome by a profound gratitude (although I didn't call it that at the time), because I realized that success whether big or small can happen in any location. But I became very befuddled by the inquiry of what determined this result? I mean how is that people can live in the same community and experience totally different realities? There are many people in African countries today living better lifestyles than people in Europe or America but at the same time, many Africans starve to death, sometimes in the same location as those who are thriving. How can this possibly be? I know how it feels to be on either side of that coin and I can assure you, it isn't some random act or accident that gives one person a great life and another a miserable one. There are fundamental principles that are time-tested and proven to yield results every single time with perfect precision. I tapped into these laws somewhat unconsciously during the first part of my success journey and so it was bumpy with major messes and more bruises than was necessary. But I have gone on to obsessively research, study and practice the principles and laws governing wellbeing and success and have become passionate about sharing everything I know with those like you, who want to become deliberate and powerful manifesters so that life can be more enjoyable and less of a struggle.

Just as there are natural laws that govern our world such as gravity, there are natural unfailing, unchanging, immutable laws that govern the invisible aspects of our existence. If you recall in the earlier chapters we spoke of the three different levels you exist in simultaneously and we went into detail of how results are created at the quantum level, not the physical level. These natural laws governing results respond to whatever is going on at that quantum domain. Basically, your mind works in accordance with these fundamental principles to lawfully manifest corresponding results in the physical world. So understanding the mind is the first part to embracing the laws of the invisible side of success. Over recent years there's been a lot of talk about universal laws and some have received a lot of media attention and hype which may have thrown people off instead of assisting them more. I know there are many laws that govern this universe and although they remain invisible to our physical senses and seem very subtle in their performance, they are extremely powerful and must not be ignored in any way. Though I cannot go into full details of the universal laws in this book, I invite you to visit my official website and get accustomed to them there or attend one of my programs that teaches universal laws. There's plenty of resources set up for you if you wish to make yourself familiar with them but I am going to state that in my opinion, the main ones that should really become a priority for you are all elaborated and mentioned throughout this book and as you are about to find out, there is really just one major one that I believe beyond any doubt you must become re-acquainted with fully because it is the one you have absolute control over. I discovered that there was a simple and fun way of explaining it and remembering how to apply it in every moment of your life. Love^2 is the tag name that has gained popularity in my circle of influence and we use it to remind ourselves what we need to incorporate in our lives daily to ensure we stay on track. What does it mean though and which law is it referring to?

The Love² formula

There is but only one great Law of life: "Energy is". Thanks to Einstein's contribution to science we have proven that everything is made of this one substance that is neither created nor destroyed. As such, everything at a fundamental level is the same but it varies in its specific form or shape depending on its vibrational frequency. There is nothing that doesn't vibrate. From the chair you're sitting on, the bed you sleep in, the rock on the street, the water in the ocean – absolutely everything is in a constant vibrational state. That means you are vibrating as well. Therefore you are a vibrational being and you broadcast vibrational signals and have a constant exchange between your individual self, everything around you and the universe as a whole. So the main fundamental law that governs your reality is that you have complete control over the Law of Vibration. The coined name Love² means Law of Vibration and the energy amplified by your level of excitement, enthusiasm and expectation at any given moment.

If you can only choose today to start managing the flow of Love² in your life, magic and miracles will become a normal thing for you as they are for me. Here is how it works: since, in your localized individual form, you are a mass of energy vibrating at high speeds packaged in that meat suit you call your body, the energetic vibrational frequency you are emitting from you is by law being received by the universe and following the lawful and orderly manner by which all things operate, it must respond by reflecting back to you an equal match to what you are vibrating. The Law of Attraction—which most are familiar with—shouldn't be sucking up your energy and attention. Just like an efficient manager, it simply ensures you are being matched up with people, conditions, experiences that equal the vibrational frequency you broadcast.

This is an "all inclusive" universe that doesn't discriminate. You are a vibrational being who has the capacity to choose what state or level of frequency to vibrate and be in. Your level of awareness will thus determine whether you send off lower or higher frequencies because what you lack in awareness will never become present in your reality. So if you say you want freedom, love, security, money, happiness and health in your life but you're not vibrating at the frequency level of having those things they will not show up. Is this starting to make sense for you? I sure hope so!

The only way to be on top of your game is to master and incorporate Love^2 into your life, but that can only happen when you've learned to direct and govern your mental attitude. Without a developed and integrated mind, you'll still be like a panicked deer in the middle of the road blinded by headlights. The beautiful truth is, with the right mindset, an expanded awareness and a resilient integrated mind, all of this will be so easy to do and results will manifest just as naturally. Although it may seem hard to control the vibration you are offering, given how fast we change as human beings from moment to moment, situation to situation, there is one sure way of keeping track of your vibration that I want to share with you now.

Emotional fitness

Research tells us that a normal individual thinks on average between 60,000-80,000 thoughts a day. That is a lot of different vibrations being offered in just one day! The idea of controlling ones vibrational environment or broadcast seems pretty impossible and draining if we have to do it through the monitoring of thought. Personally, I would go crazy if I had to do that. Thank heavens there is an easy and simple way to master vibrational and energy flow.

There is no better way to retrain yourself into a masterful life than by employing your higher faculties, developing them and using them to stabilize and strengthen your emotions. You see, the only way to consciously understand the vibration you are offering to the world is through feelings and emotions. I believe that the reason many are starving from emotional loneliness and are experiencing a lack of love is because the majority of people have neglected their ability to connect with feelings and emotions.

When we are small kids, feelings are very much encouraged. Yet, this is not done in an authentic way because we are trained by parents and guardians to behave like everyone else so that we can fit in and be appropriate. As we grow into adults it almost becomes a sign of weakness to be connected to our true emotions. So we train ourselves to suppress and conceal so much of what we feel in fear of being misunderstood or of being criticized and judged. Eventually we go into a state of amnesia and numbness. We completely forget how to feel authentically and we get used to being comfortable in discord.

I have said many times that it's been my most amazing discovery as part of my journey to see how hard it is to end emotional loneliness and the poverty of love as compared to ending poverty of food. As soon as I was able to put food on the table for my family consistently, I was good to go as a breadwinner and only got better with time. My emotional journey and finding my way back to love and freedom was an entirely different story. That's why I know that the greatest value I can be to you is to help you find the path of least resistance that will get you back into discovering this because with love as the glue holding the blocks of your life together, there is nothing you can't create, become, do or have.

If you have been to the gym, you know that it takes a certain amount of discipline and determination to release weight or grow muscles. You also know that the easier it gets, the easier it gets, especially if you do it right. I was previously in the fitness industry and still train actively for personal pleasure. Many times I meet women who see how I train and the level of intensity I am able to sustain or the number of push-ups I can easily do. They think that I am an exception to the norm. The truth is, my first time in the gym I was a sickly fragile young girl with no sign of muscle growth at all. The muscle tone, strength and curves on my body have all been designed by me over a period of time. That's why my mum and sister look nothing like me, because I designed my own body and it morphed into this stable healthy looking toned form that's easily sustainable even when I'm away from the gym for a few weeks.

This isn't luck; it is deliberate creation at its best. That physical fitness is something I replicated in my emotional and mental state. That is why I call it emotional fitness. I want to suggest to you that you can exercise and train your emotions the same way you would train your muscles in the gym or through some form of physical workout. This will not only shape them into whatever you desire, but make you the commander in charge of which emotions dominate your life. As you become more able to sustain the good and high feelings in your life unconditionally, you will guarantee for yourself that the exchange and attraction of reality that you get to experience will be to your liking. This universe is always reflecting back to you the dominant vibration in your awareness. Most women have no idea what they are emitting on a daily consistent basis.

Are you aware of the emotions that rule your life?

A sure way to test whether what you speak and how you feel match is to observe the general overtone in:

- Your closest relationships (spouse/partner/children/friends),
- Your health
- Your finances
- The level of abundance surrounding you.

If you see a great positive flow then you are well on your way to thriving as a modern woman. Perhaps you only need to fine tune some things and turn up the success volume of your life. If however, you see more lack and constriction in these areas and you feel they aren't as you want them to be, then it is time, not only to retrain your mind and exercise your emotions, but also to incorporate Love[2] into your life starting now.

Here is a great exercise to play with at this point of our journey together. Most women lose momentum and never accomplish what they want because they either start second guessing themselves, procrastinating, getting overwhelmed, finding logical justifiable reasons to quit, or just think the ideas and concepts are too simple to be the right ones for them. Someone fed the world the wrong teachings long ago when society decided that simple and easy was not the best way to approach life; and yet everything in nature only demonstrates that life—and especially manifestation—ought to be simple and effortless.

I hope you are not one of those individuals anymore. I hope that you are playing to win in life. The truth of life is that everything is actually simple and when it's not, something is wrong. Fun and play is what it's all about! You are supposed to thrive regardless of where you are, what you've chosen to do with your life, or what you currently face.

Before we move on to the next essential step in your quest to create a bigger, better, more prosperous version of you, take a moment to ask yourself the following and take note of what thoughts, feelings, ideas, images, excuses both good and bad show up. This is the only life you've got so I hope you will make it a great one. And don't belittle your chances of rewriting your destiny. Any shift that can take you out of the current life that you feel is less than what you're capable of is worth all your attention. So show up for yourself and figure out if this is really your time to shine. If it is, you will know it!

Play sheet: The simple formula and your workout routine

Three Questions in Three minutes to determine and confirm if this is your time to shine and thrive!

1. Am I truly committed to myself to go from my current life to an awesome life that is worthy of me? Have I really made the decision to show up for myself and be there for myself as I step up my game?
2. What is my emotional fitness level? On a scale of 1–10 (1- really bad & unstable 10- really awesome & stable), how do I feel now? What can I do today to start improving and stabilizing my emotional state? (Write at least one thing that makes you feel good when you think about it or do it, then go indulge in it today.)
3. What do you feel might still be holding you back from applying these practices and principles and becoming unstoppable? (Allow yourself to be candid and vulnerable. Don't skip over this part or say you'll do this later. That's part of your block right there. You need to either overcome it or seek support and guidance from me or someone of your choice whom you know who can help you overcome this part. It might be the only thing keeping you from your dream life.)

CHAPTER 13

The Sixth Essential: Enacting the Triumphant Sequence

Having you on this page at this point of our journey together is such a delight because it tells me that you are serious about having a good life and making life more fun and prosperous for yourself. It also means that you are dead-set on accomplishing whatever goals or dreams you have chosen to commit to. Thank you for finally deciding to show up for yourself and become a self-actualized individual who opts for the best that life has to give. It is my desire that you will begin to awaken to the miracles and magnificence that the universe has been orchestrating on your behalf but you haven't yet realized. To help you with this awakening, plotting a strategic route is vital and necessary. I also know that perseverance and a strong leap of faith on your end will be required because it is always going to be a bold decision to go after something unknown: something which always carries a lot of varying aspects to add the flair, excitement and thrill of life.

Depending on your level of expanded awareness and mastery of your mind, it will either be an exhilarating adventure or an excruciating one. I want to believe that you now have the ability to make the right choices for yourself. In addition, it is an essential step for you to not only **know** what you want, but to **be** what you want. As a matter of fact, until you can be what you want, it's going to be pretty challenging to manifest the new reality. This is why the famous German writer and poet Goethe said, before you can do something you must first be something. He also made a very wonderful observation on why we must all become bold in living life. In his words he made it clear that he felt that boldness has genius, power and magic in it.

Just imagine how rich and abundant your world can be once you bring to your daily life more boldness—boldness that is authentic to your nature and complimentary to your soul. That's what makes ordinary people extraordinary.

If I compare some similar traits that I have seen in the women I admire who've had a great impact on my life and made a huge difference in this world, I see that they all had a number of things in common. Mother Teresa, Audrey Hepburn, Eleanor Roosevelt, Princess Diana: though very unique and different women leading very diverse lives, they all stood out in a positive way and they all left a mark. Even today women like Oprah and Jenifer Lopez—living twenty-first century women—though diverse in their expressions are exuding the same outstanding qualities that make them top the list in their respective fields. What I have noted from all these women is that they all followed their dreams and stepped out of ordinary thinking with a lot of boldness and authentic beauty.

Whether it's the women from the past or those still alive today making a difference, take note of how bold, beautiful and blissful they are. This is the true mark of a successful woman. Today, more than ever, we need women living in this state and demonstrating to others how deserving every woman is of a life they love living.

Being a more confident, abundant, happy and healthy version of you is what you must first focus on before you take any major physical actions. There are four main feminine types or roles that I have found every woman plays in her life. Unfortunately, because they are rarely taught or emphasized anywhere, they are more often than not applied in the wrong sequence delivering unwanted results. Over the long run, this has increased the conflict and ill conceived beliefs and ideas regarding a woman's success and place within society. I hope we can to put an end to this starting with you.

* **The first is the Doing Woman:** Every woman always has lots to do and a lot of responsibilities weighing on her from family, children, spouse, house chores, professional responsibilities and the family pet: the list is endless. This is the most commonly known role and is what almost all women are struggling to keep up with today, all focused on effort and physical actions. Nothing is wrong with the doing woman or being a woman of action when it is the proper and inspired action instead of the sacrificial daunting one that most endure on a day-to-day basis.

* **The second is the Enjoying Woman:** Generally this disappears once you take up relationship and family commitments. It's also the hardest for most women because someone managed to convince us long ago that it's bad to just allow ourselves to enjoy. A feeling of guilt and shame or unworthiness is always attached to this role so very few women indulge in it. We see more often than not that as a woman seeks out love, financial independence and family she gives this aspect of herself up. Today's woman barely has time to enjoy anything, including food! Guess what the kids have also picked up from their mums? You guessed it! The same. Every evening when I pick up my child from school I see all these young kids rushing with their mums, food in one hand, attempting to eat, while running as the other arm is being dragged by the mother who always seems to be running out of time! And I am always wondering, "Where is the fun in that? It looks so miserable." I have no idea if the child's mind is on the food, the running or the place they are rushing to. It's really hard to see how any mother who practices the art of thriving would desire to put herself and the one they love so dearly in such a panicked state. Of course every woman in the world wants only the best for their loved ones but enjoying is part of ensuring that they have the best. This is something many women have forgotten completely. It's so erroneous though, because every woman needs downtime, play time and fun time in whatever way appeals to her—whether it's dancing and some nice champagne like me, or spa time with girlfriends, cooking classes or whatever gets you juiced up.

With that should also come the retraining of how one works with time! Contrary to popular belief, time isn't an ultimate reality. It is a perceptual, relative event that every individual can understand and work with better to their advantage. Enjoying the action or activity is just as important as accomplishing it. The more calmness we can bring into our daily chores the better we will become at demonstrating and living in that elevated state of feeling blissful. That's also the only way our children can pick up the best behaviors to adapt into their lifestyles as they grow up. It sounds like it's a lot to ask when I say you need to find a way to make your daily routines more enjoyable and relaxed, because everyone associates enjoyment and relaxation with vacations. But you're not going to go on vacations every week! So isn't it wiser to bring that essence of vacations into your everyday life? Enjoy life more, it's the only way to bring in more good stuff. Being in that fun, restful, carefree space is something many women today deprive themselves of but it must be incorporated into the lifestyle of the modern thriving woman.

* **The third is the Being Woman:** This one has almost been drowned out by today's fast paced world. I wish to point out that this role presents a double-sided picture for your consideration. I am encouraging you to take up this role by first being grounded yourself and discovering that stillness that lies within you which is the powerhouse of your feminine energy. Next you radiate the energy and emotions of the person you wish to become. Very few women today take the time to just be, to find their stillness, and center themselves. Most women leap out of bed in the morning and spend the whole day in internal turmoil and an endless "rush hour" all day every day in an attempt to control the uncontrollable and solve the unsolvable from a state of instability and confusion. If you are sitting in the problem, there is no way the solution will come to you, even though it's already there. Only in a state of being can you enact or apply yourself to anything well enough to impact your life. Taking time to center yourself every single day before tending to the needs of others no matter how tiny they might be (newborn babies included), is a gift I encourage you to give yourself starting today. There are many tools and processes that are available to help you so just make yourself familiar with one that suits your taste and begin today. There is

never a better time to change your life than now and the fastest way to set the wheels in motion is through being in that calm, quiet, grounded state along with vibrationally, emotionally being and feeling the woman you are desiring to become. Being must become a priority in your life should you wish to change your reality.

With that brief description of the different role-types we can be as women, the modern thriving woman does not choose amongst the three, she simply balances all three feminine role-types in her world and harmoniously executes each one to experience holistic and meaningful success. You don't ever have to choose between being, doing and enjoying because you ought to express them all effortlessly! You never have to choose between a girl's night out and meditation, or family time and quiet time because you can be, do and enjoy them all. It's in having it all that you will find the satisfaction of being, doing and enjoying. But the sequence is everything. You must follow the right sequence and commit to yourself to keep at it no matter how chaotic your world may appear to you. Trust me when I say that with time, everything will fall into place once you find your own stability. As with everything, practice makes mastery. If you feel yourself to be a victim in this life then it isn't because you can't be the master but because you have not yet shown yourself that you can be the leader and commander of your own life. Take charge, create your balance and everything will respond in accordance to that newfound state.

How do you know what the right sequence is for you? Remember these key words: **"Before you can do something, you must first be something."** That means that the dream you wrote down at the beginning of this book is finding it's way toward you and it'll get to you really fast if you first become the person you know you would need to be in order to live and own that dream as a practical reality. Becoming only happens first and foremost in the role of **"being"**. Hence in every moment make your starting focal point the role of **Being – Doing – Enjoying** in that sequential order.

As you gain more proficiency in being and learn how to effectively do it, the right sequence will become your natural pattern of co-creativeness in all your activities. The best part is that connecting yourself in your own being-ness is summoning the creative energy that powers every manifested thing. As you practice being what you want to have, inspired action becomes the natural spontaneous impulse. You cannot help but take action, but not just any action—you take inspired and bold action. This is the best way to take up the role of Doing. Once you do, confidence and positive expectation will be pervasive and you will naturally expect the outcome you wish to reach you. Enjoying everything will be a natural by-product for you in your life and every day you will find yourself radiating this beautiful glow of how much you love your life. It really is that simple and you can absolutely make it happen in your world. Life is awesome and if you still doubt that just give these concepts some serious testing and let the universe show you what you've been missing out on all this time.

Another way of looking at the sequence that I usually teach in my mastermind groups that you can get details on if you just email me or visit our website should you feel that you need some support is through the following guidelines for manifestation:

Assumption – Alignment – Action – Attraction.

This has been by far the easiest way to teach anyone how to become a powerful manifester and the good news is, if the first two A's are accurately done, the last two are guaranteed to produce the manifestation. In essence, it is the same concept, just different angles of approach and whichever feels simpler and more in resonance with you I urge you to put to the test. I know we haven't spoken of alignment prior to this and in the next chapter we will dig deeper into its relevance for you in this journey. For now, soak in this particular chapter and let yourself become a bit more playful and childlike with the idea of enacting and being what you want to see manifest in your world.

I want to share with you a great secret to bring this baby down to a nice landing. Though I am not religious I am aware of the sacred scriptures of the holy Bible where creation and God is first spoken of and after a lot of research and study with great spiritual teachers and interpreters of this wonderful collection of holy scripts, I believe with all that I am that everything we have shared together in this chapter is validated in the Bible. I want to invite you to re-read the chapter on creation with the new expanded awareness that I hope this book has given you. Looking at God and the sequence by which creation emerged with a fresh pair of eyes and an expanded sense of awareness, I know something new will be sparked in you. I certainly hope you will be kind enough to send me a note and let me know how different things feel for you, now that you have a new fresh take on life, manifestations and your potential.

The main idea here isn't to change the current conditions you have physically. Let God and natural laws take care of all that. This is why Action or doing isn't the first thing to give your attention to. Rather, revert back into the sacred space of your mind that we've been taking about and begin there. Be what you know you will be once your manifestation is here. See it, live it, become it mentally and emotionally first and saturate your entire inner world with that essence and let that be what dominates your thoughts, feelings and behavior. What I am saying, if I am saying anything, is that this version of you that you feel you deserve to experience doesn't have to be "out there" any more. It can all come and be "in here" right now and your mind is not only capable but willing to show you how easy it is to change your world. So if you struggle with health and want to have a good body and feel beautiful and sexy, you have the chance right now to become as beautiful as you can imagine yourself to be. If you want to experience peace, happiness and know what bliss is, begin now to see and feel yourself blissful and in complete serenity. If you desire to have love and feel confident and secure or abundant in your life, allow yourself to let it be now and imagine how you will feel and what you will look like – but live it in the now. That's the same way everything was created, even in the Bible. Everything God made was first imagined in the mind of the creator after which it was made manifest and above all,

God enjoyed every bit of it. You are made in the image and likeness of God. Perhaps it's time to learn a thing or two about the sequence he used for creation and employ it in your own creations. After all, as a woman you represent the feminine energy of God's ability to birth and make manifest every visible thing. Your true authentic power and gift lies in how much awareness you hold to realize the truth that has now been revealed to you. The trumpets will be blown in celebration of your revelation and discovery of your own genius, power and magic. I am absolutely excited and grateful that you are this close now to your greatest life experience yet!

CHAPTER 14

The Seventh Essential: Perfecting the Art...

The only way to perfect anything in life is by doing over and over again the thing itself. So if there is such a thing as perfection in our human life, I believe it must just mean taking inspired action, practicing it numerous times and seeing it through till the end result is achieved no matter what the topic may be. The fallacy of waiting for something to be just right or conditions to be perfect before you make your decision or act, is one of the best breeding grounds for procrastination and self-sabotage. I strongly recommend abandoning the idea of your life conditions first becoming perfect before you can pursue the things you dream of whether it's bliss and balance in your life or something more tangible. With all that we have revealed so far and the new understanding that I hope you will carry with you from now on, it's natural that most of the time when you embark on your new dream things will appear far from perfect. And that is perfectly okay once you initiate from the right starting point. Since everything is always vibrating at a specific speed and frequency whether it's your physical body, the earth spinning on its axis, the sun or all the heavenly bodies on the cosmos, your life conditions will always be in constant motion and either create more of what you don't want or more of what you really want. The determining factor will always be you and your level of awareness and mastery over your creative abilities.

We have mentioned many important concepts and steps to ensuring that you begin thriving in your life and harness that prosperous state of being that's found in bliss, beauty and abundance, but we have one last crucial element that must be added into this chart of plotting guaranteed lifelong success in life. That element is **Alignment.**

Though you may find many testimonials of people and ideas from individuals of how success can be attained and ways to go about it, none of it guarantees whether or not you get to attain it yourself. Recently I was invited to a small gathering where a network marketing company assembles their members to encourage and motivate them so they can keep working hard. They bring in a few cases that already are successful to give testimonies on how great the product and company are so that those still struggling don't despair. I was asked to speak a few words, given my well-known ability to instill hope in people's lives and make them feel good. Although I am not a fan of the term "motivation" because I doubt it ever produces any real lasting results, I do believe in inspiration. As such, it's always a pleasure for me to voluntarily allow spirit to flow through me and fill others up with the great gospel of love, joy and prosperity.

Before commencing my talk, I sat there listening to these wonderful men and women who had created great success stories and earned significant financial abundance doing so. I ended up changing my entire speech because something in me called me to speak of the very idea I am about to share with you now. It is one thing to hear of success stories and get systems that are strategically built to work, but listening, following or imitating those who portray success—especially in financial terms—still does not promise you will have the same result even if you physically do everything they tell you. Why?

The invisible laws that govern success can only be tapped and accurately harnessed at an individual level and this requires total alignment above everything else. It is alignment that integrates and brings everything together in natural harmony for the full manifestation to occur. Very few know this and even fewer have learned how to align and integrate themselves in this world. For the one who finds alignment in their life, it doesn't matter what the subject at hand is, they will manifest exactly what they wanted or something better every single time. So whether the manifestation was releasing weight and gaining a new body image, or attracting a companion and soul mate or even something more materialistic like a pile of money or a promotion—they always manifest it and many times it appears to the uninitiated as luck, good fortune or the right connections and so on. In truth, it is the fact that they have perfected the art of alignment and thus the art of thriving in every domain of their life. What I am saying is that for you to fast track your new self image and begin to experience more harmony, bliss and prosperity in your life, you must find your alignment. This was my message to the group that I had the privilege of talking to. Once the alignment is there, the resources, information and systems that are offered will produce the desired results. If there is no alignment, it will always be a struggle to attract the clients or money or the soul mate. The body will just not shape up no matter how much exercise and diet you subject yourself to or which celebrity trainer you hire and that work promotion will keep going to the guy sitting next to you. I hope you are getting what I am saying here: **alignment is everything!**

Have you ever listened to someone tell you how their whole life changed after trying just a simple training course or attending one seminar where someone just said one single statement that turned their life into gold? They might have been attending a three-day event and only one statement brought the magic for them. But here's the thing, although that information was important in helping with increasing awareness, the Midas touch came from the inner alignment that was achieved by the individual. So right here you have the opportunity to gain your own Midas touch and transform your entire life in the most fun, simple and effective way ever, just from this very tiny and simple book. That is, if you can tap into this art of aligning.

What is this alignment and how does it work?

The fact that you exist in more than one domain is something you need to begin taking into serious consideration as you go through your days. As I said before, you are a three-part being localized in a dualistic world. The confidence and boldness or beauty and bliss that you wish to begin expressing in this material world must come from your highest domain where duality doesn't exist. So starting from the field of pure potentiality that you emanate from, whatever you desire to express that is progressive and expanding in a fuller way is already done at that level. That is why Jesus Christ said, "Ask and it shall be given to you." I want to restate it and say, "It's always given to you." However, you might not be in a position to receive and interpret it because if your other two domains are clouded and corroded or out of alignment (which is the case for most people), the full manifestation will be disallowed by YOU. Not by someone or something else—always and only by you. Granted, they might be blocks that you picked up from other people and circumstances, but in every case, unless you have some attachment and agreement with the block itself it cannot be in your vibrational atmosphere.

Let me give you a quick example of what I mean. If you have a fight with your partner and he says "no" to something you really desire so your energy drops and you get emotionally devastated, the desire doesn't remain unmanifested in your life because your partner said no or didn't support it. The conditions surrounding your desire might not be conducive from an external perspective and so you might blame him or finances and other things for never living out your dream. But the fundamental truth is that your dream wouldn't be realized because you consented to the opinion and judgment of your partner and the rational conditions that you saw, thereby keeping your vibrational frequency at a different level from that of the manifestation. Wow! So you asked and it was given from that higher domain of your soul or spirit, but you were so busy being stuck in the wrong problematic frequency that you couldn't be receptive to its revelation. You can blame your partner all you want—for the rest of your life if you like—but at the end of the day, only your vibrational offering determines what you can or cannot manifest.

I see many women still in the dark with this, precisely because the idea of alignment isn't taught by a lot of people. Everyone is too busy selling the money or car or some other end result but not so many people have had to seriously start from scratch as I've been fortunate enough to experience in my life, so they miss out on the subtle yet key elements that keep the gap wide and overwhelming. Today, you have the chance to create a turning point in your life if you choose to align yourself better. The idea is to create your own love story where all three levels of your existence are in love and harmony with each other. At the quantum level or the level of your mind is where you have the most awesome power of effecting this change.

For many women, the quantum leap of their life seems impossible because they are emitting two different frequencies. You see, while your dream is always possible and already created at that spiritual level, unless your mind (which is dualistic in nature) is able to realize and interpret it turning that formless creative energy into a tangible form, the desire will remain stuck on the invisible quantum side of your existence. Only the mind has the power to either allow or disallow this natural creative process and that has everything to do with the mental attitudes and paradigms held. So how you work with life and your mind is really the only reason why what you want is still not falling into place. If you don't have that alignment incorporated into your activities and endeavors, life will keep serving you exactly where you are even if it isn't where you want to be. The crazy awesome thing about your mind is that not only is it dualistic in nature but it also holds the capacity to split energy in such a way that on the one hand you can have a part of you that loves the new idea and desires while another part of you (your paradigms) prefers to have things as they are because it's familiar and less risky. So think of it like this: at the Spirit level you might be dancing to symphonies of classical music but at the physical and emotional level you might be dancing to crazy techno music! I take pleasure in using these two analogies in my own life because it helps me keep track of my own harmony. Clearly you can imagine how chaotic it would be to be playing classical harmonious symphonies with the current techno trans-type of music on the same tuner at the same time. No one would want to be anywhere near that tuner, right? Well, imagine what's happening with your loved ones and clients when that happens to be the case with your mind!

To bring order and clarity into your life is the beginning of alignment. Only the mind can cause the split in energy and vibrational offering and only the mind can resolve it. Once there is alignment at the quantum level, the physical level will automatically follow suit and all the manifestations will pour forth as naturally as a flower blossoms. I once read a really powerful statement that I want to share with you which helps bring some relief when I find myself expanding into new horizons and notice my split energy. The statement says, " The day came when the risk to remain tight in a bud was more painful than the risk it took to blossom." The split energy experienced as you cross over from your current level of awareness to the higher but yet unknown level will shake you up and cause discomfort, but you will have the power to overcome it and bring both harmony and results into your life through alignment.

It can take a really long time to get there or a relatively short time but it all depends on you and how well equipped your mind is. Have you noticed someone you know who attained the level of success they wanted but it took them decades before they could manifest? I bet if you asked them how long it takes to manifest what they've got they would tell you it will take however many years it took them. This is not accurate though because there are also many who've attained a lot of success in a relatively short amount of time without struggle. What gives? Well, for the person who needed decades to manifest—that was the amount of time it took for them to come into full alignment and allow in the solution or desire. For the individual who took very little time, that was the period they needed to come into their alignment. That's it! So imagine how different your life could be if you could perfect this art of alignment and become proficient at coming into your alignment on the subjects that matter most to you.

This art of alignment cannot be overlooked at any cost and the mastery and application of it opens up the kingdom of heaven for anyone—especially you, my dear reader. Pick yourself up in this moment—emotionally, mentally, spiritually and physically—and trust that you can find a way moment by moment to create your own love story where only one harmonious dance is happening with great passion and enthusiasm. Then watch the momentum carry you into the depths of great beauty, bliss, prosperity and a life you absolutely love.

CHAPTER 15

Boosters for That Bold, Beautiful, Blissful Experience

Just as there are tools and equipment that help a builder construct, a chef cook or a hairdresser style hair, there are tools that we all possess which can help us master the art of thriving and feel more in control of our reality. So far we have focused on understanding the mind, its functionality and the process by which the formless takes shape in physical reality. We outlined the different essential steps that you need to take, did some emotional and mental workouts to get those mental muscles and higher faculties back into shape, and even played a few games. If this has just been the first time you have heard about all these different ideas, then please be loving and easy with yourself and enjoy the journey because as long as you do not stop, you'll get there.

I can do any kind of push-ups in the gym today, from regular ones to dumbbell push-ups and reverse push-ups. All of this was at one time a dream for me because of how frail I used to be. When I began, I couldn't do on-your-knees push-ups (girly push-ups) at all! My bones and muscles were just not strong or developed enough to carry out such a heavy task but I had a desire to be healthy and fit like the female tennis players. Even though I can't call myself a tennis player I can assure you my vision was achieved. I never stopped training, strengthening and growing my muscles. At times things appeared very hopeless and I felt more comfortable stopping because it didn't seem like anything was happening physically, but because I found a way to keep going it all paid off. I live the experience I once envisioned in my health and wellbeing, my relationships, my lifestyle and every other area that's important to me.

You can bring into your reality and daily experiences a lot more than you've settled for so far and I think deep within you there is a great yearning to do just that. Although I don't know what your specific desire is, it's certain that if it is a true desire you can make it your new way of life. To help you better apply everything we've discovered so far, as well as track your progress so that daily occurrences can feel less like random mysteries and more like synchronized clues and signals from the universal mind trying to guide you, I want to make you aware of two extremely powerful tools for designing and building your dream life.

Attention and Intention

Nothing can help you become a deliberate controller of your emotions (which happens to be the only language that the universe understands) than your focused attention. Deliberately focusing your attention on what you want and how you want to feel is the biggest service you can do in the process of manifesting your dream. It is the only thing you have total control over—although as human beings we've become so lazy with our thinking and focus that in the beginning it feels unnatural to focus on something contrary to what's in your surroundings. But that is exactly what you must do, especially when seeking to manifest more self-confidence, abundance, joy and wellbeing. Very often when we begin this journey of following our dreams and living our best life, it is in the midst of the absence of the desire. So looking for serenity and harmony tends to start in the midst of chaos and confusion. Happiness, joy and bliss tend to be in the midst of depression, anxiety and unhappiness. Robust health and wellbeing tend to be in the midst of an unhealthy situation and so on. This isn't a bad thing. This is your life and your destiny calling you and speaking to you, wanting you to utilize your creative capacity to let in a new way of life. Believe it or not, the very problems you feel keep you from a life you love are actually the way that life is daring you to be bold enough to follow your heart and listen to the signals around you, so it may express itself more fully with and through you. It is your purpose and destiny seeking to shine through and express a higher version of you that perhaps you don't even know exists. It is, in other words, beauty, love, health, abundance and bliss seeking to express and expand in a higher and more satisfying way than you've had so far.

So you want to begin blessing those problems in your reality now and you want to pick up your tool of attention and use it on overdrive because what you place your attention on will expand. As that expansion and energy becomes focused and concentrated on the thing you want, intention is the universal intelligence transforming that energy of attention into form for you and with you. So if attention is concentrating energy together to flow in a specific direction, intention becomes the information and details that will inevitably solidify that energy field into manifestation. Whether good or bad, it will work to serve this purpose and the commander, director and determiner of all this, is you and how you use your mind through thought-power and emotions. Harness these two tools and use them in service of your dreams rather than in an attempt to eradicate the unwanted. If you want to feel more confident and bold today, pay attention to the direction you give to your energy and align your attention and intention to be on the feeling of already being confident, secure and bold rather than the avid awareness that you are not yet. Therein lies the secret to fast manifestations.

Gratitude and Appreciation

This would be a very incomplete book if I did not share with you the importance of gratitude and appreciation when it comes to boosting yourself into a thriving reality. What many still do not understand is that life isn't about suffering or struggle. Only those who live in ignorance of the great truth of life need to struggle their way until they find the truth and master it. You have made your way to the place in time where the clues of your life are speaking to you in so many ways: through your longings and your discontent, through the daily experiences you have (both good and bad) and via different avenues universal intelligence is attempting to communicate with you through and guide you. For example—this book you're reading now!

Nothing is random or accidental in this world. Everything is intended here by a higher domain power and it is all meant to aid you. An observation that was made which helped change my thoughts and viewpoint of the world was stated by Einstein who said, "The most important question a person can ask is, 'Is the universe friendly?'" Earlier in life, I think I was having a hard time placing myself in this world or trusting that life could really work out for me because I always felt like I was battling some unseen force that didn't like me at all. You know what that feels like? When you feel so small in a great big ocean and you have no idea if anyone is watching out for you?

After encountering that statement, I chose to retrain my thoughts and anchor in the idea that above all else, the universe *is* a friendly place. What that meant for me was that I could trust and let go more. I could relax more and quit trying to control the uncontrollable or force things into happening because at the end of the day, I am living in a friendly universe that wants nothing more than my progress and wellbeing. You must ponder this idea and make a decision, too, because it will become your anchor in rewriting your destiny. If you can truly know and believe with all that you are that this universe is only intending to guide you into more harmony, more prosperity and a fuller expression of your joy and beauty in whatever way you wish to express them, then you will never again be swayed by naysayers or people who lost their connection with the truth of life. Gratitude and appreciation is the tool that will unleash this knowing for you rapidly. If you can find even a little glimpse of hope right where you stand now and be grateful for that, it will become the peephole that leads you to the doorway that ultimately opens up more things that you can be appreciative of. If you become a hunter for the little good in your life every day, that's what you will continue creating and after a while it will hit you that you no longer justify your success by the amount of struggle and hard work you do because you understand success is your birthright. That is thriving at its best and that's what life is calling you toward now. Not just for you individually, but everyone in your circle of influence and your world at large. Thriving isn't just about manifesting the stuff you think you want in order to be happy and enjoy life. It's about reaching a higher level of living where bliss is to be found and abundance flows unimpeded as you share the best of you and demonstrate the unique gift you came with into this world. This is my deepest desire for you and it is my expectation that this small book has just helped in revealing to you the path that will lead you there.

The Three Stages of Gratitude to Reach for

While we all know across all holy literature and wisdom traditions that gratitude is expressed as being one of the most important things anyone can do to put themselves in good favor with the powerful Source they believe in, it is rarely mentioned how to effectively perform gratitude. I was having a conversation on gratitude and appreciation with my daughter where I was trying to sell her the importance of taking just five minutes a day no matter what's going on, to perform gratitude. I asked her to give me an example of how she does it so far and she told me, "I say things like, 'Thank you for my health.'" I told her how wonderful and perfect that is, but I was reaching for something more specific and so I prodded her a little more which she wasn't too happy about because she wanted to go and play some video game instead! Nonetheless, I wasn't going to let her off the hook until she gave me an example of what she meant when she said, "Thank you for my health." And that's when perhaps one of the biggest lessons ever was revealed. She thought about it for a second and said, "Well, I say thank you for my health, meaning, I'm happy I'm not sick and I don't have a cold like most of my friends." And I went on to share with her how out of harmony that gratitude was, because expressing appreciation of health by pointing out the unwanted is simply training yourself over time into an unwanted vibration. If you can remember the simple formula of Love^2, the vibration you broadcast which is tied up in the meaning and emotion you hold at any given moment is what universal intelligence will respond to. So in the case of my daughter, being grateful for not being sick is a lower vibration that would amplify, gain momentum and eventually manifest itself. So I helped her gain the understanding that every subject always has two contrasting signals potentially existing simultaneously and it was up to her to align with the accurate one. Only through "feeling" can we effectively determine which is truly in alignment with our soul and highest good because one will always feel good while the other won't. Thus I had her sit for a while and learn to "feel" the gratitude and meanings in her words so she could connect better with this practice in a beneficial way. Shortly after that she realized that saying, "I am grateful for not being sick", is very different from "I am grateful for my healthy heart and beautiful strong legs." One feels really good and the other doesn't.

It requires conscious training for each one of us to connect with our emotional guidance system and remember how to think, feel and act in harmony with what we want instead of what we don't want. Social conditioning has us trapped and numbed out of this simple yet profound understanding and so as you make gratitude a ritual in your world, be sure to be relating yourself with a higher positive and aligned emotional output and not the automatic default that we've inherited. Most of the time it's pointed on the lack!

So, there are three main stages to master as you make gratitude your new way of life and I will simplify them in few words and allow you the opportunity to expand on each as you wish.

Stage One

This is the easiest and most preached stage of gratitude. It is being grateful for all the good you already have in your life now and in the past so that more can keep flowing. Teaching my daughter to be grateful for her healthy heart and strong beautiful legs is a great example of this first stage because she's already got them going for herself in the most perfect way. Anyone who can think and speak can master this quickly.

Stage Two

This second stage requires more awareness and wisdom because it is at a higher level of understanding. It will stretch you but after having read this book, it should be a challenge you easily conquer because you will quickly connect with its benefit in your world. This level of gratitude is giving thanks for all the good you have in your life as well as the bad! It's what Jesus spoke of in all his teachings and it certainly means you have made peace and reached a level beyond ordinary human awareness to effectively practice this stage. In practical terms it means that you can honestly sit down for a few minutes and feel thankful for the apparent darkness in your world, or the pain in your body, or the loneliness in your heart from being single. It means practicing unconditional love. But here is where I want to digress a bit because most people think that they need to look at something awful in their lives and force themselves to feel love and appreciation. Far from it! It means that you go beyond your ego dominated thinking that only holds a dualistic limited perspective and align with the perspective of your spirit. Then you will see beyond the pain and connect with the already inherent pleasure contained within it, because as we all know, one cannot exist without the other. So if you are living in a reality of poverty or sadness or illness, knowing and connecting with the truth that there is an aspect present of an equal and opposite nature to that which you are part of and capable of tapping into, is what will allow you that unconditional love. Although you might stand in the midst of illness, it will not shake your mental and emotional strength because you know there is a way to manifest wellbeing since there is only one Source. This is the perspective that Spirit always has and it will be your ticket to employing this level of gratitude and awareness. As you become a master at these two stages and you naturally learn how to surrender and flow with the changes of life, the last stage will come with ease.

Stage Three

This is the heightened stage of enlightenment. Every sage, seer, wise teacher lives and breathes this level of gratitude. In my opinion, it's easier to attain it slowly as the other two become mastered. This stage is when you become grateful for simply existing. It's becoming one with the universe and everything in it. It comes as a result of completely abandoning the reign of the ego-mind and living profoundly from a state of enlightenment. When you give thanks just for being, you don't say "I am grateful because I am so healthy and happy and I can't wait to have that car or that home." None of that! You simply say, "Thank you" because you exist; I am grateful today because I am here—period!

I have no idea how practical it is for me to only live from this state because I also like to enjoy a bit of contrast and expansion in my life, but I have learned to do my best to create more moments in my days where I get to bask in this stage of gratitude. I must confess, with all the distractions, addictions and pleasure seeking activities I have done (and I have tried a lot of things in my life), nothing has ever felt as good as it feels when I allow myself to get in the zone and connect with Spirit and my highest sacred self in that profound way. It is the most magical feeling you will ever experience if you can only give it a bit of practice in your life. This is gratitude at its best and it is the biggest booster you will ever give to the unfolding of your dreams.

Play Sheet: Boosters for that Bold, Beautiful, Blissful Experience

••• Take a few moments and consider a topic that you are having trouble with, then apply the simple exercise of feeling through your emotions whether you are focused on the having of it or the absence of that particular thing. Notice where your emotions are pointed: if they feel good when you talk and think about it, then you're emitting the right signal, but if they feel bad then it's because you're emitting a signal of lack which will only create more of the same.

••• What 3 things can you be grateful for that you have in your life today?

••• Pick one situation that is awful and causing great discomfort in your life and rather than resisting it or picking out the badness of it, see if you can sell yourself the idea that you live in a dualistic world. As such, the equal and opposite experience to what you have is also present at the quantum level if only you can tap into it. Now allow yourself to find some relief from this experience by releasing the resistance and finding thoughts and feelings that make you feel like it's not too bad where you stand. Envision the extreme opposite of that situation and feel for a difference and a shift in your emotions even before any physical action happens.

This is learning the mastery of deliberate creation and shifting reality! Using the tools of attention and intention, do your best to think up at least 3 good things that could come up as a result of this particular experience. Surely you can find 3 things, no matter how deep in the hole you are.

Remember, we can only see the stars when the sky is darkest!!!

Art of Thriving as a Modern Woman

DAILY GRATITUDE LIST

1. _____

2. _____

3. _____

4. _____

5. _____

6. _____

7. _____

8. _____

9. _____

10. _____

Be still and quiet for 5 minutes
CONNECT WITH YOUR HEART AND FEEL
OR SENSE LOVE AND COMPASSION.
SPREAD THIS FEELING THROUGH YOUR ENTIRE BODY...
THEN MAKE AN INTENTION TO SHARE THIS SAME
LOVE AND COMPASSION WITH 2 PEOPLE YOU CARE
ABOUT AND 1 PERSON WHO TROUBLES YOU.

SEND ALL OF THEM A GLOWING BALL OF
LOVE AND COMPASSION ON THIS DAY.

CHAPTER 16

In the End...

At this point in our quest you are as ready as you will ever be to become the author of your life. Nothing will make real sense or even prove to be worth anything unless you put it into play. Words don't teach, only knowledge and experience that will come through practice—if you begin now. There will never be a perfect moment for you to start something new and life will never pause or slow down for you long enough to allow a new turning point. The basic law is that everything is either being created or disintegrating. So, in this moment you are either going to move upward in your spiral of creation and expansion or you'll move downward. The power of choice lies with you and I feel I have done my best to simplify the tools, concepts and skills that are necessary for you to steadily and rapidly spiral upwards into a new reality.

I started off without the hope of ever experiencing anything meaningful or joyful in life and I worked off my perceived handicap day by day. At times when it was really tough I just took it moment by moment. The desire to live a better life, to experience happiness and joy, to feel like I have value and that I have something more in me to give to the world than just problems and poverty is what led me to this moment in my life where I am in love with all of me. I wish the same and even more for you, not just because I understand your struggle so far, but more because this is your true nature and something you most definitely deserve. I really want you to connect with that, because there is a huge difference energetically. To come from a place where you choose to master the art of thriving and opt to live life boldly and in total bliss simply because it is your true nature is very empowering and draws in more things that match these feelings because it doesn't feel like you are attempting to have something that doesn't belong to you or something you've never had. It feels like a return home; it's in fact a remembrance of what you knew before you were taught to speak and act like other human beings. This is your birthright! That's the approach you need to have with this matter and that's why you owe it to yourself to reignite your true essence before your last day on earth.

The next time you look into the eyes of a baby, notice how complete and content they feel. They are always in total bliss and I have never come across a baby that isn't beautiful and radiant just as they are. They do everything with complete confidence even if it's the simple act of crying and getting attention. I am sure you can connect with these words, right? Well let this serve as a reminder of your goodness, innocence and capacity to connect to that very power that produces this miracle we call a baby. You are the same miracle you know, just overgrown and overdressed in costumes and social masks and make-up that led you to believe that you are not. Getting back to who you really are and living the life that is worthy of you is the best service you can give to the world. As you find this alignment, none will benefit more than your loved ones and more so, your children.

The more I find myself and align with this higher power that flows through me and reveals ideas and materials such as the one you're reading now, the more I understand my role as mother. I have always felt that there is very little I can give to my daughter because I don't know how to advise on most of the social benefits and preferences that those who haven't grown in poverty consider normal, such as school stuff, homework or even the kind of university one should aspire to attend. Although knowledge and education is one of my great loves, I didn't get the chance to formally pursue it. I have no family stories to share with her and school projects on family trees are always a downer for me because I just don't have what normal families in her school have. From a social perspective it would appear as though she's at a disadvantage, yet she stands as one of the most brilliant children around in every area of her life. The credit can only go to the Spirit that guides my life and hers, which enables me to learn and enhance my own alignment and thrive in my life. This is exactly what I share and teach my daughter today and I have discovered beyond a shadow of a doubt that the best gift any mother could give their child is alignment.

If you can show your children how to align with their own Higher-Self and their Mind, they will have at their disposal the resources and energy that creates the world. Never again will they struggle their way to a goal or get swayed by opinions, criticisms and beliefs that aren't beneficial to them. They will naturally lean on the upward spiral of positive creation and life will not be a hard mystery for them but a wonderful adventure with great scenery instead. I can see now that what we need to focus more on is teaching our children how to "be" and how to align because as they master that, the rest falls into place automatically.

This is the great promise that alignment and successful living carries for you. It has served me well in my life and I have countless stories that I could give as an example of the impact it's had on the lives of those I tend to, but I feel that you have caught the spirit of my words and that you'll certainly put it to the test to see just how much brilliance you can spark from those you look after once you show them how to align. The only precursor to this of course being that you first and foremost teach and show yourself how to align and perfect it in your world and manifest your dreams because you can only give what you already have. The biggest lesson from my whole life experience has been the true demonstration that I have shown myself and inevitably those around me that fate is what life hands you but destiny is what you choose to do with it. Thus your destiny awaits you regardless of the fate life has dished you so far.

Closing the Gap: What if I am still Fearful and in Doubt?

The choice you've made to rewrite destiny and build your dream does require you to go the distance and reach untapped horizons. It will soon become clear to you as it did to me that a gap gets created the moment you start going after your dream life and there's a period in your life where you find yourself in this gap between the "what no longer is" and "what is not yet". This is very normal and part of the transition and transformation as you reach for your new life and results. There will always be the death of the old to give space for the rising of the new and I guess because no one really talks about this gap, most people get there and assume it means failure. So then they retreat before the dream becomes a physical reality.

Shed some light on this gap today and understand that this space between what no longer is and what is not yet is indeed the sacred space where you get to transform and become all that you need to become as the owner of that dream. That space can be used to push you into success or pull you down into failure. There can be the fuel of love that comforts and guides you and directs and helps you pick up the clues life is handing you so you can cross over faster. On the other hand, fear can reign and block out love which would then send you on the opposite side of abundance and surrender to your higher self.

Noticing how you use this gap and maintain the right focus while still in that space will be part of your becoming and self-actualization.

Should you get caught up in that space as most people do, find any possible way to get back on track and build the confidence and the bridge necessary to make the cross fast and as enjoyable as possible.

One of the things I encourage and promote often that I picked up from Dr. Michael Beckwith is the term MSU. MSU stands for Making Stuff Up! If you can use this space or gap that is guaranteed to happen during your creative process to make stuff up in a powerful and beneficial way, then fear, doubt, overwhelm or despair will not find their way into the sacred mental home where your dreams are cooking. Certainly bliss, clarity as well as an ever increasing confidence and unshakeable faith will be your daily experiences and the most amazing part about discovering how to best manage that gap between the old life and the new dream is the core of thriving and success for any individual. Until and unless that gap is beneficial and nurturing, the journey of success and the art of thriving will remain a tale told by others. Enroll in MSU and you're guaranteed to thrive.

For many people, doubts and fear will still sneak up from behind and try to sabotage their efforts. We have all had days when we wake up and just feel like the world is falling apart and everything is going awry. Women tend to give up a lot faster than men, because being very sensitive and emotional creatures, we find it too overwhelming or wrong to deal with negative feelings. Here are some words of comfort that might help when those days show up and I guarantee you they will especially help in the beginning as you cement this new belief system.

- Allow yourself to feel negative emotions. Do not block them out or condemn them just because you're a student of personal development. A lot of people get it wrong when they think that the art of thriving means you never have to go through sadness or anger again. Quite the contrary! Happiness exists simultaneously as sadness and the embracing of both with constant focus upon the good emotion rather than it's opposing equal is the optimum state of living. If you want to reach that state of bliss and happiness you must go up that ladder of emotions, and depending on where you've been living so far, the initial climb might require a few stops at frustration, disappointment, and maybe even irritation while you make your way upward toward hopefulness, optimism and so on. The vibration of anger and that of appreciation are so far off that you will need to allow that progression to take place. Allow it to come through and utilize the power of your mind. Direct and govern it toward the desired state, but in no way suppress any emotion, because if you suppress the negativity, you will cancel out the positive feelings as well. Just feel, breathe and keep progressing toward the mark.

- Gain a better understanding of what fear and doubt really is. What you need to know is that your mind is only here to process and interpret life into the best and most realistic version that it can but it's all very much dependent on the paradigms held by you. Everything that manifests or doesn't manifest is actually only happening for your own good. Many continue to rely only on the local or ego mind though they know it not, and as such they have a very limited scope of what is possible for them. If you've been falling victim to this up until now, then chances are as you start to expand your awareness and pursue a bigger, better life, your localized mind will cause a split energy separating that harmonious alignment with the universal mind. It is this gap that will haunt you and build clouds in your world that make it seem as though there is no sun.

When fear and doubt come up as you go after your dream, go outside and look at the sky on a cloudy day. Let that be your reminder that the sun is always shining above the clouds and notice that the clouds are always moving. They aren't permanent and neither is your current feeling of doubt or fear. You can assist its rapid progression into more certainty by building your confidence through the effective use of your mind and true knowledge of the principles governing your wellbeing. That way you get more proficient at applying the principles and practices that help you close that gap and get back total alignment. I believe this book has provided enough ways to get you there and should you still find trouble closing that gap then be bold enough to come and join us in our worry-free, doubt-free environment where we will support and nurture your dreams into life. There is a worry free diet that you can start on today, but just putting fear and doubt into proper perspective gives you enough relief to allow their dissolution.

There's nothing wrong with experiencing fear and doubt as you retrain and re-program your mind. It is a bold step that most wouldn't dare.

They would rather have the comfortable misery that they have made a way of life than a new temporarily uncomfortable unknown that could eventually become a new heaven on earth. You are a rare breed and I am so happy and grateful that you have chosen me to be your partner as you continue to uncover the great treasures life has to offer. I am honored that you have shone your light on this day and embraced the fact that it will be a bit scary and uncomfortable, that some days will bring doubt and fear, and it will feel uneasy and unusual and probably be unpopular among your peers. In spite of this, you've decided that you love yourself and life way too much not to take the risk. What you will notice as you keep going from here onwards is that it's more than worth it because the impact, the love, the difference you will bring to your world is a legacy worth dying for.

Remember this one factor through everything that you embark on now and in future. Nothing meaningful, lasting and fulfilling will ever be created without a foundation of love. Every change, each new endeavor or discovery that you will hope to accomplish successfully and with ease can and must come from a place of love. It is the glue that holds everything together in this world. It is why I have dedicated my life to sharing and giving my best in every way I can and it is also what the world is in dire need of, as the experience of lack and a deficit of love in many aspects becomes more prevalent. The transformation for you will happen rapidly and in a joyous fashion if you can love your way through it all. Find symbols, reminders and slogans that help you incorporate that loving, kind attitude toward your own self even in the face of your own negative aspects, as they make way for this new emerging you. Love is the only way to cast out all negativity without destruction and it is the only healer I found to work in my life. Remember love in all you do… in the end, it's all that you need to heal, transform and manifest the reality you wish to experience.

CHAPTER 17

Putting it into play

You have come to a moment in time where the rubber must hit the road. So far all we have been doing is gathering, discussing, dissecting and relating information. While all the above is necessary for one to attain knowledge, it's still mechanical and results cannot really show themselves in your reality until the knowledge is fully internalized and implemented by you. Therefore, despite the fact that we are at the end of our time together in this particular context, may it only be the beginning of something brand new that turns your world around and brings back the vitality and enthusiasm for life that you once had or have been dreaming of.

As you go forth now, dreaming bigger dreams for yourself, allow the flow of life and the power within you to lead the way and switch off the volume of past thinking or patterns of limitation by turning up the volume of abundance and wellbeing. Gain enough courage to be the commander of your life and give others their proper roles in the movie of your life. It isn't about getting rid of anything or anyone that doesn't please you but about being so focused on bringing to life the state of being that you wish to experience that every person and condition has no choice but to change in your favor or dissipate from your experience.

You and I live in an attraction-based vibrational universe. There is no exclusion at all! Therefore there is also no such thing as separation, it's simply an illusion-based perception that you have power over. So whether you are being justified and rational when sorting out the good from the bad, your attention to the bad is still doing you a disservice because it will keep the good you want away from you and bring more of the bad that you certainly don't want. So be easy on yourself as you master this art, and understand that above all else, it's your true nature and you just need to shed off the paradigm blocks that have prevented you from being your best Self.

In the Vedic teachings there is a term for manifestation that applies to all of nature. This term is "lila" or "divine play". According to this ancient wisdom teaching, everything in creation happens in a natural and playful way. I have taken the liberty to investigate some of nature to see if this was accurate and, sure enough, I even came across documented proof that dolphins (which are ridiculously smart animals) best learn when trained through playing. I don't own a dog, but I am aware that dog training has to be a playful game for them to get maximum results and quite frankly, even watching a lion hunt looks like a calculated game to me. I have come to the conclusion that the best way to retrain your mind and manifest your desires faster will require you going against the current wave of thinking that still believes successful living and thriving means serious, arduous business. In fact, it is literally counterintuitive to what your parents may have told you about life itself —but nonetheless it stands to be the secret truth held by nature. Add a lot more fun energy as you engage in this process, make it playful and trust that self-actualization is natural to you. Thus, it can only be divine play that will always feel good and be simple to undertake.

Take off the lid in your life and embrace the idea of living from a place of love, joy, grace and boldness. You are as beautiful and as blissful as you allow yourself to be and it can all come into your experience no matter what you've manifested in the past. Your family, your colleagues, your community and those whose lives you touch will benefit greatly once you have this as your daily living. I don't know about you, but nothing gives me more satisfaction than effortlessly being at my best and knowing that I am of benefit to someone else.

This is your next point of action

Remember, nothing is worth anything until you apply and gain true knowing of it, which in turn must automatically yield results. The biggest decision you now have to make that will determine what you bring into your world over the coming days, weeks, months and years is based on your power to choose wisely. There are fundamentally only two choices. One is to choose statically and the other is to choose dynamically. Being a static choice maker will keep your awareness constricted and attached to the past, which is bound to get you creating more of what you've already had in the past. However, I want to encourage and invite you to be a dynamic person from now on. Being dynamic means you love and embrace the new and fresh flow that life is always presenting. It means being in your own flow, focusing on the present and being flexible and open. That is where you will tap into all the power you need to rewrite destiny. It is as Charles Givens once said, " To design the future effectively, you must first let go of your past." That's exactly what you need to do if you desire a fresh start with a brighter future. Making a conscious choice to be a dynamic thriving individual is what will get you everything you want and more.

The subsequent steps will now summarize the best steps that will move you closer into the full realization of a new thriving version of you. As you hold on to your desire or goal and stretch yourself to reach for that state of being bold, beautiful and blissful in all your experiences, it is necessary that you now incorporate the following:

1. Make a Serious Commitment to Yourself

It is time to make that decision and really stick to it. Many women aren't attaining the level of success they deserve because they suck at keeping their own word to themselves. To thrive, you need only make the decision and keep at it no matter what.

Go from the good life to the awesome life as a woman and put everything we have learned in this book into practice. If it feels too overwhelming or hard to begin on your own then take the next step and reach out for support and help from the right people. I don't really care whether you choose to work with me or find someone else that better suits your taste. All I want is for you to put it into play and stick with it because I know it can work for you. Be there for you because life will only show up you when you first show up for yourself.

2. Figure Out Where You are Now

Charter your course starting where you are now so you can begin moving in the right direction. No more happy face stickers, sweeping things under the carpet or trying to be socially appropriate and unselfish by sacrificing your own wellbeing for the sake of others. There is no greater injustice that you perform to yourself and the world in general than that of living and giving less than your greatness. But your greatness will not shine through until you align yourself the right way, with all the different aspects. So you need a handle on the paradigms you hold, the emotions that dominate you, the thought patterns that populate your mind and the self-imposed limitations that have kept this dream you have away from you.

Begin by gaining awareness of things like: Do I feel seen? Do I really feel loved? Do I feel worthy of a life better than what I currently have? Why and when did this start?

You've got to name it to tame it because so many women have become invisible even to themselves and are kind of numbed out. If this relates to you in some way, you really want to get in touch with yourself and know yourself again.

What has led to this silence and muting? Write out just 7 things that come into your awareness now.

Know yourself and feel yourself starting with where you are now so you can become what you want to be, do and have.

3. Connect with Your Higher Power and Shift Your Perception.

Live an empowered and inspired life, and leave behind the tarnished clothes of social conditioning and common thinking. So many women are living a disempowered life that is ultimately a lie because they buy into the idea that things can't get better for them given their current circumstances. Nothing could be further away from the truth. But to gain freedom from this requires a raised conscious awareness and a mind that is governed, directed and controlled deliberately.

Everything I have shared with you in this book has been an attempt to evoke enough curiosity to seek the path of wisdom, truth and abundance. It may not be the most popular book as it simplifies everything and speaks of promises that many human beings have been led to believe are impossible on earth, but I didn't write it in search of popularity. I wrote it in search of you and in service to you. The desires you have been carrying within your heart that seem to be dying have a way out and you hold the key in your hands now. Your mind and the capacity to utilize the aspects we spoke of in the precise manner that I detailed out for you will give you constant and direct access to powers greater than you and I can currently imagine. But you must understand the journey and know that this is a personal path that will be unique to your unfolding and along the way you will be required to grow and expand more. You will need to uncover and replace your limiting beliefs and paradigms and completely shift your thought patterns and strictly secure your emotions and feelings so that the personal actions and behavior you're involved in produce only the desired outcomes. None of that is possible without a powerful, well-orchestrated mind. The mental adjustment you make will very well determine your capacity to connect with the Source of all your goodness. I choose to believe that you are on fire and all set to step out boldly, beautifully and remain blissful throughout this marvelous journey chosen by you.

Conclusion

Growing up in destitution right in the bosom of poverty and a feeling of unworthiness meant that I had to figure out some remedies to get me through each day or perish in anguish. A tale that greatly inspired me in life and helped me fight my way out of my darkest days was that of Cinderella. Though I didn't have the privilege of owning the book itself, I was introduced to the story because I happened to temporarily steal it just to read it. My love for books and for the beautiful enchanting character who got her happy ending against all odds took me farther than I ever anticipated. Today I am the proud owner of numerous limited special edition Cinderella dolls and movies—all of which I offer no apologies for even at my age, because I feel in retrospect she somehow helped me tap into my own flow and align with universal laws and find the path to manifestation. I didn't know it consciously, and wasn't able to fully articulate what I had done in my life that was so different from what all the other slum kids around me did. But today I understand that it must have been a mental adjustment that Cinderella inspired out of me, which aided me in keeping a "die hard" attitude going. Since I was only a few years old, that eventually got me through every horrible job (and I have had the worst kinds), illness and poor health, bad relationships, the sense of failure that came with my inability to gain formal education and on and on—the list is just endless. If it didn't kill me, I found a way to keep holding on and Cinderella, that poor, unwanted girl who had nothing good in her life except music and unusual friends who would comfort her, played a colossal role in my life. Today I live my happily ever after and my love for shoes may have just sprung up from that tale as well, who knows?

It's important that you take all the clues that the universe uses to speak to you because it never uses the human language that we're accustomed to. In the midst of our most trying situations are concealed clues that would help pave the way for the greatest success ever if only we align ourselves precisely. The lesson from Cinderella isn't just about the happily ever after, but the fact that she always had control of her mind, she kept the long-view and strived to make the best of what she had. She had a very powerful mind that was focused only on what she wanted and in directing her mind and designing her dreams, music and love were her constant companions—as they have been for me too. The situation may seem futile, but you always have power over what to make out of your life and you can always focus independent of anything around you. When you do, it will become evident to you that magic and miracles or fairy godmothers don't exist only in the realm of fairy tales. They may be in different forms or shapes, but they can be found right where you stand. If at the very least this book does nothing at all to catapult you into your greatest success, let it be the first clue that will lead you into your version of heaven here on earth.

There's an outstanding true story of a woman that I was fortunate enough to hear just recently that I feel depicts how having the right mind-set, heart-set and alignment can truly change anyone's life. It also shows the commonality of deliberate creation and how anyone can create the same happy ending that both Cinderella and I have experienced. It is of a woman whose name remains anonymous, but I will share with you that she lived in America in the 1950's and at the age of eighteen she was married off to a husband, which is what had happened with her mother and grandmother. But she was one of those square pegs trying to fit in a round hole. She could feel that her heaven on earth was possible no matter what her current reality was. In her heart lived a burning dream to travel the world and live life fully as a woman. However, her reality included a mean husband, who eventually took off and left her a couple of years down the line with five young children. Just imagine being in your twenties after having given birth to five kids consecutively and playing housewife to a man who thinks you're just household furniture, then being abandoned suddenly while carrying such tremendous responsibility! Surely life was more like an unending nightmare for her.

Somehow she pulled herself together and found a way to get through each day in serious survival mode with her five kids. In an era where women still had no voice or sense of value and freedom, she held on to her dream of being free and able to travel the world some day. I believe it was this dream that kept her going and inspired her to find a way to make ends meet. This woman made a decision to be a dynamic individual and chose to do something that changed her whole world and set her up for a thriving life. She chose to save just one dollar each day, and she collected it in a coffee can that was hidden at the back of her closet where none of the kids would ever see. Every single day, she made sure that she put a dollar in that can no matter what. Now, one might say it was selfish given her situation and the fact that they were struggling. But in truth she was being and doing what every woman must do—follow their soul's agenda. In all honesty, she knew that her family was always in struggle mode so sparing a dollar a day wasn't going to break them anymore than they already were. Coffee can after coffee can, this lady kept her dream alive and although it would be twenty years before she could realize her dream, this lady was able to travel the world and finally enjoy the fruits of her being and doing. This story was recited by her grown up daughter who went on to become a very high-spirited and successful individual as well. I share this real life success story with you because I want you to see that although life can hit you hard and send you to the bottom, you can still pull yourself together where you are and little by little climb your way to the top. Even if you can't see how joy and abundance or that dream you have can be pursued and attained immediately, just begin with the little you have and keep the long view if you have to! Neither that woman, Cinderella nor I had any idea how it would all turn out, but we kept at our dreams and we did the little we could where we stood. There is always something new that you can do where you stand now—even if it begins with a coffee can—to move you closer to that life you know is worthy of you. Now, it may have taken women who were big dreamers longer in the past because no one was sharing and inspiring and supporting each other and this kind of material was hidden from the public, but now you stand in a different position with everything easily accessible. There couldn't be a better time for you to create a life you love living and I hope with all my heart that you find yourself worthy enough to give yourself that gift of true freedom.

The reality of living with courage and a knowing that a power greater than you is always moving with and through you is more liberating than any physical freedom you might be seeking. The good news is that as you find that higher level of mental and spiritual freedom, the physical freedom must manifest too. You were born to express radiant beauty and to enjoy your life and share the very best of you with others. The perfect miracle that you have manifested as, which is this physical body that contains more cells than there are stars in the galaxy, is proof enough that only the best belongs to you. As you become it, live and share it, you will see that thriving is your true nature and that being bold, beautiful and blissful doesn't just make U better, but the entire Universe.

About the Author

Janette Getui is a lifestyle and wealth Psychology Coach that works with women internationally to help them bring more balance, joy and beauty in their world. Being born in a Kenyan Slum in Africa, she has taken on and personified the perfect phoenix metaphor, demonstrating that anyone can recreate their life and choose their destiny against all odds. She's a published author and writer for several magazines and she helps many individuals achieve and create exponential success through her numerous trainings and programs. Although she had very little formal education, this self-educated, self-made mother and entrepreneur has had the honor of both being trained by and working with some of the biggest names in the personal development industry as well as some of the greatest cognitive science teachers of our time. She truly believes that her life's purpose and meaning is to share with others the simple methods and concepts that bring more order, riches, harmony, beauty and love to each of us and the world in general. She eagerly shares a path to a better quality of life that is authentic and full of beauty, bliss and love with those who resonate with her very often unique, elegant, bold and fun way of teaching. Every woman deserves to live the modern life on her own terms and enjoy successful living.

Meet Janette at: www.janetttegetui.com

For more bonus awesome resources and downloadable gratitude pads go to: www.boldbeautifulblissfulu.com

Printed in the United States
By Bookmasters